Schilder: Preserver of the Faith

Rev. Henry Vander Kam

VANTAGE PRESS
New York

FIRST EDITION

Copyright © 1996 by Rev. Henry Vander Kam

Published by Vantage Press, Inc.
516 West 34th Street, New York, New York 10001

Manufactured in the United States of America
ISBN: 0-533-11637-6

Library of Congress Catalog Card No.: 95-90592

0 9 8 7 6 5 4 3 2 1

Contents

Foreword

During the last few years, several of my colleagues in the ministry of the Christian Reformed church have urged me to write on the life and times, the influence and theology of Prof. Klaas Schilder. I had also often thought of doing this, but the time-consuming work of ministry in the churches and a large volume of denominational work made it necessary to delay this project until after I retired.

I had been enamored of the thinking of Professor Schilder for many years. My appreciation for him increased greatly after I acquired, read, and studied the bound volumes of *De Reformatie* from the year 1920, the first year of its publication, and through all the years of Schilder's editorship (1929–52), until 1962. What a wealth of material! It was a goldmine of the best Reformed theology and a journal of the history of the Reformed churches in Holland for that period of time.

My purposes in writing this volume are two in number: (1) making Professor Schilder and his contributions to the Reformed faith known to English-speaking people, and (2) to make clear the history of the Reformed churches in Holland to the same audience so that they see their own churches in the light of the history of the Gereformeede Kerken in Nederland (GKN) and are warned about similar pitfalls in the life of the churches today.

True, Professor Schilder is known somewhat in the United States and Canada through his masterful trilogy on the suffering of Christ, translated by Dr. Henry Zylstra and published by Wm. B. Eerdmans Publishing Company. Zylstra has performed an important service for Reformed people. Four years ago, Dr. T. Plantinga published a translation of Rudolf van Reest's two volumes, titled *Schilder's Struggle for the Unity of the Church*, published by Inheritance Publications. Plantinga, too, has left many Reformed people in his debt. But Schilder wrote so much more that has not been translated into English. He is a theologian worthy of study by the whole English-speaking Reformed community.

The history of the GKN during the past fifty to sixty years is naturally of interest to Reformed Christians in the United States and Canada because their roots are in those churches. The GKN was greatly blest with able theologians and a faithful membership for many years. Somewhere things changed radically because we no longer see the strength and faithfulness of those churches today as they were some years ago. What went wrong? Was Professor Schilder responsible for the split in the GKN? Many think so, and those who hold this opinion have little respect for him. Others, including myself, have a different view.

This little volume is sent into the religious, and especially the Reformed, world with the hope and prayer that it may teach the reader something about this eminent scholar and warn the churches against the errors made in the GKN. I dedicate this book to my beloved wife of more than fifty years, Elaine, who has been my encouragement throughout my career. May the King of the church use these efforts to the praise of His name and for the welfare of His church.

Chapter 1
The Historical Setting

In order to see the story of the Dutch Reformed churches and Klaas Schilder in proper perspective, it is necessary to first sketch the history that led to the circumstances of these churches in the early twentieth century.

The Protestant Reformation and the Confessions

The momentous Protestant Reformation of the sixteenth century had a profound effect on people in their religious lives and, essentially, in all aspects of their lives. It gave the Bible into the hands of the common people, and in this book they found the comfort they sought as it guided them in their thinking on all of life's problems. A new day had dawned. Prior to the Reformation, there was a pronounced gap between the officers in the church and the ordinary members. The rich and the poor inhabited the land, but there was then no middle class. Politically, the masses did not count because they were without knowledge, and all the orders came from an elite group at the top. The benefits of education were closed to the lower classes; consequently, they were not able to leave their "chains" and better themselves. The church had not attempted to enlighten the people, and, as the ancient prophet said, they were "destroyed for lack of knowledge" (Hos. 4:6).

True, salvation came to light with the coming of the Reformation, but so much in addition was accomplished by the movement. Because the people had been held in ignorance for so many years, the leaders of the Reformation movement soon began to prepare written materials so that they would be able to enlighten the common people. The most famous reformers, Luther and Calvin, wrote numerous articles and pamphlets on a host of subjects. Luther's greatest contribution in this field was perhaps his translation of the Bible into German. Calvin wrote the first edition of his *Institutes of the Christian Religion* when he was only twenty-seven years old.

Several authors wrote catechism books so that there would be some material for the instruction of the youth in the church. Calvin was one of these writers. It is true, there were no confessions written yet, but catechism books based directly on the Scriptures were used. Definite confessions not having yet been made, it was very difficult to judge the teaching of any one of the many teachers who arose during the early days of the Reformation period. These facts, together with the differences that had arisen among the reformers on points of doctrine (for example, their understandings of the Lord's Supper), made it clear how necessary it was to have confessions in the church that would bind all of the membership together in a common view for a common purpose.

The first of the Reformed confessions outlining Calvin's views of Scriptural teaching appeared in 1561—only forty-four years after the beginning of the Reformation. It was written by Guido de Brés and is referred to in the English-speaking countries as the Belgic Confession. The creedal document deals with the various parts of doctrine, later called the *loci* of dogmatics. These *loci* deal with the Belgic Confession doctrines on God, humanity, the person of Christ, salvation, the church, and the last things. In other words, they pronounce on all the articles that Reformed Christians believe in their system of doctrine. Such a confession proved to be most precious to the people of that day in that it provided clear answers for them as they debated with others on various points of doctrine.

Only two years after the Belgic Confession was written, the Heidelberg Catechism made its appearance. Even though Calvin had written some catechism books and many other able authors had done the same, the Heidelberg Catechism belonged in a class by itself. It had been commissioned by the Elector Frederick III, of the Palatinate and was written by two comparatively young men, Zacharius Ursinus and Caspar Olevianus, who arranged biblical teachings from the point of view of human sin, the salvation of humanity, and the life that is required of those who believe. The outline for the catechism derives from the systematic arrangement in Paul's letter to the Romans, and through it the authors showed concern not only to teach theology but also to provide genuine comfort for Christians.

This catechism, too, was originally intended for the youth of the church, but when the young people received instruction from it, the parents often stayed to listen because it was all new to them as well. As a result, after only a few editions, the catechism was divided into fifty-two "Lord's Days" so that the ministers would be able to preach on this material on every Sunday of a year. It is difficult to judge how great the influence of the Heidelberg Catechism has been, but many Reformed believers have repeated the words of the first question and answer—words that state what is their only comfort in life and in death—in their dying hours. Preaching on the catechism has brought a certain balance and comprehensiveness into proclamation in the Reformed churches. The catechism calls for treatment of many subjects a minister might otherwise omit. Wherever the catechism was faithfully preached, the church profited greatly by its pastoral instruction in biblical truths.

The Reformation Comes to Holland

Although the leading pioneering reformer Luther was from Germany, and Calvin, though born in France, spent most of his life in Geneva, the Reformation came to the lowlands at an early date. This area became perhaps the most important place for the development of the Reformed faith. Holland had struggled for eighty years to regain its freedom from Spain. A war that spanned generations naturally wreaked havoc in the lives of the populace. In the war that lasted from 1568 to 1648, Holland came out as the victor. The residents of the small country had fought valiantly and were fortified by the Reformed faith, which put steel into their souls. The leaders as well as the common people embraced the teachings of John Calvin. In the lowlands the gospel according to the Reformation was placed in direct conflict with the teachings of Roman Catholicism, and the former carried the day. It was mentioned earlier that English speakers call the major work of Guido de Brés the Belgic Confession. In Holland it is known as "the Netherlands Confession of Faith" because Belgium was a part of the one country, the Netherlands, at that time.

Even though various other churches sprang up in the Netherlands, the Reformed churches have always held the dominant place. The royal family embraced the Reformed faith; their action was one of the factors in establishing a state church at a later time. The existence of a state church brings problems of its own, but these difficulties were not considered too great in Western Europe in those days when many countries had a state church. Later such establishments would produce all kinds of difficulties. The United States, of course, began with the firm conviction that there ought to be no state church. The complete separation of church and state is also not an ideal solution, since it so easily becomes a separation of state and "religion," an idea few people would endorse.

The difficulties attending the improper relationship between the church and the state surfaced early in the seventeenth century. Leiden was the home of one of the theological schools where the Reformed ministers of that day received their training (the others were located in Groningen and Utrecht). At Leiden a bitter debate broke out between two professors—the more conservative Franz Gomarus and the more liberal Jacobus Arminius. Gomarus held to the Calvinist view that salvation is accomplished by divine grace alone without a human contribution, while Arminius believed that humanity did play a role, however small, in working out its salvation. The debate went on for some time—much too long for the welfare of the church. It soon became evident that only a national synod would be able to make a proper ruling regarding the matters at issue. But for some time the ruler refused to call a synod together and his permission was required. Not until 1618 was a synod convened at Dordt-recht in Holland. The synod was ecumenical in character because the delegates came from several other countries as well as the host country. It was really far too late to call the synod together because Professor Arminius had died several years before the synod met in 1609, with the result that his point of view had to be represented by someone else, Simon Episcopius, a very able spokesman for the teachings of Jacobus Arminius. The synod met for a total of about six months, from November 13, 1618, until May 9, 1619.

Important matters were handled at the synod. First of all, it had to deal with the immediate occasion for its convening, i.e., the dispute between Gomarus and Arminius. Professor Arminius had drawn up five statements that were the center of the dispute. Briefly stated, they were:

1. Conditional predestination, that is, predestination based on God's foreknowledge of who would believe.
2. Universal atonement in the sense that Christ's atoning work was sufficient for the salvation of all, although some resist it.
3. Saving faith, which can be attained only through regeneration and renewal by God.
4. Resistible grace.
5. The uncertainty of perseverance (summarized from

Philip Schaff, ed., *The Creeds of Christendom* [sixth ed.; Grand Rapids: Baker Book House, 1990 (reprint of 1931 edition)] 517–19).

The synod rejected his teachings and in each instance took positions that were the direct opposite of Arminius's contentions. The five statements adopted by the synod have become known as the *Canons of Dort*:

1. Divine predestination in the sense that election is absolute and unconditional, not founded upon foreknowledge.
2. Limited atonement in that the efficacy of Christ's saving work extends only to the elect.
3. Total depravity.
4. Irresistible grace.
5. Perseverance of the saints (summarized from Schaff, 519–23).

Although adoption of these theological points became its most famous contribution, the synod did much more. It elevated the Belgic Confession and the Heidelberg Catechism as well as the *Canons of Dort* to confessional status, something that had not been done before. The synod adopted a "church order" for the Reformed churches by which they were to be governed. Besides this, it adopted a liturgy for the churches. A group was appointed to translate the whole Bible into the Dutch of that day. The synod, though it had to overcome the difficulties presented by having members from several nations, managed to perform an enormous amount of work. One of the consequences of the doctrinal position that it adopted was that Leiden was purged of Arminian teachings so that the Reformed faith, as taught by Calvin, could flourish.

The "Fathers of Dort" considered doctrine to be very important indeed, and they were not about to have someone teach a theology that, in their opinion, neither the Scriptures nor the Church Fathers approved. They underscored the biblical teaching concerning the sin of humanity and concluded that by nature people are totally depraved. Yet there is an unconditional election by which God has chosen a people to Himself, not on the basis of their works, but only by His grace. The atonement through the blood of Jesus Christ is the only way to the Father and the only way of salvation. This atonement is unlimited in its power, but God has restricted it to those whom He has chosen. This grace of God cannot be resisted by people. It will always triumph! Those who are brought into fellowship with Christ in this way will continue in the faith that they have been given and have confessed. In the Canons the delegates to the synod summarized a wide range of scriptural teachings; they also ordered that the Canons as well as the Confession and Catechism were to be respected and believed.

The creeds adopted by the Reformed churches at Dort have focused the minds of church members on the central features of God's revelation, and in doing so, they have kept the church on the road it should travel. In the view of the delegates, no one has the right to play fast and loose with the confessions. These statements, though they were authorized by human beings, make up the formula of unity in the truth. Office bearers in the church were required to sign a formula of unity by which they pledged that they accepted these formulations and agreed to be judged by the clear teachings contained in them.

Slowly the church made progress during the rest of the seventeenth century. It had a good foundation, and many of its leaders built well on that base. However, at the dawning of the eighteenth century, it became evident that the internal problems of the past together with some of the difficulties brought in from the outside were causing the church to go into decline. The old problem of church-state relationship did not go away, and several movements that had arisen outside the country left their influence on the church. The deism of England, the German Enlightment, and French atheism all had their effect on the welfare of the church in Holland.

Holland is a small country that occupies a geographical position among several European giants. England to the west and German and its predecessor states to the east have always exerted a great influence on Dutch thinking. Deism, the Enlightenment, and atheism produced a brand of preaching that by traditional Reformed standards could only be termed sterile. What the church had gained in 1618 was to a large extent taken away from her in 1816 by royal edict. Parts of the *Canons of Dort*, specifically the negative statements, were set aside by the state church, and it dropped the church order that had been adopted by the Synod of Dort. It appeared that the church was going to go through a very difficult period, and indeed it did.

The theological schools were taken over by those who had no love for the Reformed confessions. Ministers preached on all kinds of subjects that they considered timely, but in the minds of many, the gospel no longer rang out from the pulpits. A number of church members became very discouraged and began to wonder where they could go to receive what their hearts needed. Although some were deeply concerned about developments in the church, the majority failed to discern the gravity of the situation and dropped off into a profound theological slumber.

In general, these were the conditions in the Dutch church especially during the years from 1816 to 1830. The glory of the Reformed churches had departed. It seemed to some observers that if current developments were to continue much longer, there would, humanly speaking, scarcely be a church left.

A Time of Secession and Renewal

Some of the greatest poets Holland has produced lived in the early part of the nineteenth century. Some of them, especially

Isaac Da Costa and Bilderdijk, began to write about the sad condition of the church of that time. Bilderdijk exercised a great influence on the literate public. But it was a simple young minister in a small village in the northern province of Groningen who gave decisive leadership in trying to do something about the ecclesiastical situation. This minister was the Rev. Hendrik De Cock of Ulrum.

Few would have chosen a man like De Cock to lead a reforming movement in the church. He could hardly be called a deep thinker or great pulpiteer. He was the minister not of a large city church but of a small village congregation in the middle of the farmland of Groningen. Nevertheless, leadership was thrust on him; he certainly did not seek it. He simply preached the gospel of Jesus Christ and upheld the traditional position of the Reformed confessions. His preaching on sin and grace was enough to distinguish him from the neighboring ministers because their sermons did not center around the gospel. As a result people started coming from considerable distances to hear De Cock preach, showing how hungry they were for the truth of the Word of God. Soon parents who had children to be baptized and who did not want their own liberal ministers to baptize them took their children to the worship services at Ulrum so that De Cock could administer the sacrament of baptism to them. The Ulrum church was filled to capacity at every service.

What De Cock was doing soon became known to the neighboring ministers and to the church authorities. They did not find his highly successful ministry a model to be emulated; rather, they became angry with him and took steps to silence the only man who was bearing witness to the truth in their area. They were able to appeal to a rarely enforced legal point in their handling of De Cock. He was soon arrested, in November 1834 and again in 1835, because he had violated the stipulation of the Napoleonic Code that no more than nineteen people could gather in any one place at one time—another indication of the hold the government had on the church. He was jailed and fined. He and the members of his congregation were desperately poor so that these added financial burdens proved impossible for them to bear. Besides, although the impoverished parishioners had scarcely enough to eat themselves, soldiers were now quartered in the homes of many of them, and they were compelled to feed their unwelcome guests.

There were times when De Cock nearly despaired of life itself, but he always found strength in the truth of the Scriptures. Many of his letters from prison have been preserved, and in them he pours out the distress of his heart.

After a period of time, De Cock discovered that he did not stand alone. Several very capable ministers took up his cause. A sizable group of theological students also rallied to his side. These men began to realize that the greater part of the preaching in the church of that day was totally unsatisfactory. What would be the future of the church if a man with the principles of Hendrik De Cock, rather than being applauded, became the object of persecution? Several men who became prominent later on now took the side of De Cock; examples are Brummelkamp, Van Velzen, Gezelle Meerburg, Van Raalte, and Scholte.

Because De Cock and his supporters found the situation in the state church to be intolerable, they seceded from it in 1834. From their action the movement received the name *de Afscheiding* (= the separation/secession). To be more precise, De Cock himself did not actually leave the church; rather, the state church expelled him from its ministry. The group that followed him out of the established church was not large, but there were enough people so that he was able to continue ministering to a congregation.

In the preceding period, many members of the church had eagerly sought out his preaching, yet, at the crucial point, most of them stayed with the declining national church, since leaving the state church also entailed substantial social, political, and economic consequences. De Cock certainly welcomed the leaders who came to his side, but they would probably not have been able to give the initial push to the movement that he had given. As noted above, even the Napoleonic Code adopted in Holland provided a legal pretext for arresting De Cock. However, the church that came out of the secession of 1834 was soundly Reformed, and through the secessionist movement, the honor of Dort had been restored. People would now hear the full Calvinist gospel preached in the newly independent churches.

In 1854, only twenty years after the secession, the Kampen theological school was founded. Some training had been taking place in the parsonages of several ministers, but now a full-fledged theological training could be given to the prospective pastors. The theological school began with no less than thirty-seven students, most of whom came from the parsonage training program. There was a marked contrast between Kampen theological school and the three theological schools of the state church. At Kampen, the Scriptures were recognized as supreme, and the confessions occupied their traditional authoritative place. There may not have been the same level of scholarship there as there was in the three older institutions, but the churches that supported the new school were convinced that the preaching that resulted was far superior to what was heard in pulpits of the state church.

The nineteenth century saw another group leave the established church. If the secession of 1834 spoke mainly to a simpler and less educated class of the church membership, the second "secession" included some of the best minds of the country. Dr. Abraham Kuyper, who became the central figure in the second secession, had been a graduate of one of the older theological schools and had served as a minister in the state church for a number of years. Although he was a pastor in the Hervormde Kerk, he was far from Reformed, and he even called his youthful faith into question in later years. But God had a purpose for the man.

Several events in his early life shocked him in his unbelieving attitude. He read Charlotte Yonge's *The Heir of Redcliffe* and was shaken to the depths of his soul by the calm faith of which this novel spoke—the sort of faith he had not experienced. He studied the Polish Reformer John a Lasco and was deeply moved by his faith and zeal. In the first church that Kuyper served as minister—the church at Beesd—a simple, uneducated lady, Pietje Baltus, spoke to him of her living faith, and he realized that with all his learning and natural abilities he did not possess what she had. God used simple means to accomplish a radical transformation in him. Once Kuyper saw the light, however, he unleashed his vast energies and talents in a new direction.

In 1880 he founded the Free University of Amsterdam because he was convinced that the universities of that day did not meet the standards that Kuyper thought Reformed institutions should attain. He himself taught at the new university for some years. However, he came to realize that having a better institution of higher learning was not enough. The church itself had been corrupted by a spirit of secularism, and the higher critical approach to the Scriptures had made deep inroads. In 1886, six years after the founding of the university, he led a large group of like-minded members out of the state church. The movement that he led came to be known as *De Doleantie* (= mourning)—the feeling that Kuyper and his followers had regarding conditions in the established church in which they had been born.

The Secession (*Afscheiding*) of 1834 had restored to those who supported it a sense of confidence in the church and its leaders. They found that they could now worship in a church where they knew the word of God would be proclaimed. The *Doleantie*, though echoing the same basic views as the movement of a half century earlier, spoke to a different class of people. Many of the educated and prominent people of the time joined forces with Dr. Kuyper. The *Doleantie* also had a broader perspective on what the implications of the Gospel were for the Christian life. The adherents of the more recent movement emphasized Christian education, Christian politics, Christian economics, and Christian journalism. That is, it had a broader vision of the kingdom of God than the earlier secession. The far-ranging kingdom vision was something new, but a novelty that was also very appealing to many who thought deeply about such matters. As the Kuyperians saw it, the word of God shed its light on every phase of life. Consequently, they believed that Christians must labor with that word in every sphere or area of life. The life of the Christian is made more complicated in this way, but it was also far more rewarding.

As a result of the secession in 1886, there were now three parts or divisions of the Reformed churches in the Netherlands. There was still the state church, which was by far the largest of the three; there was the group that had seceded in 1834; and there was the segment that had followed Kuyper out of the state church. The one group (the seceders of 1834 and their successors) had established the Kampen theological school and the other (*De Doleantie*) had founded the theological school that was a part of the Free University. These differences in groups and theological centers must not be overlooked; they will surface again and again in later years. However, the two groups that had left the large state church held to the same confessions and the same basic teachings. By all appearances they belonged together.

In 1892 there was a merger of the heirs of the *Afscheiding* of 1834 and the supporters of Kuyper; the result was the formation of a denomination that chose the name *De Gereformeerde Kerken in Nederland* (= the Reformed Churches in the Netherlands; it will be referred to as the GKN). Not all the members of the two secessionist movements approved of the merger. One group, consisting of individuals who especially opposed some of Kuyper's positions, declined to join the merger and instead formed yet another denomination, which tried to outdo their former colleagues by calling themselves *De Christelijke Gereformeerde Kerk* (= the Christian Reformed Church).

The merger of the majority of the members of the 1834 and 1886 groups was not without its difficulties. It soon became evi-

13

dent that some of the theological understandings in the one group differed from those in the other. For example, Kuyper taught the doctrine of presumed or assumed regeneration by which he meant that a covenantal child is assumed to be a child of God until and unless the opposite becomes evident in his or her life. The 1834 seceders did not accept Kuyper's position. This point and other differences were brought to the denominational synod in 1905, which met in the city of Utrecht; the result of synodical deliberations was a document entitled "the Conclusions of Utrecht." Various points of doctrine were discussed, and a *compromise* on the question of presumed regeneration was reached. It is important to remember the decision of the GKN synod of 1905 regarding the issue in order to understand the history of the denomination a few decades later.

While the 1834 and 1886 groups chose the route of secession, there were also members who were genuinely dissatisfied with conditions in the old historic church but were not willing to leave it. They preferred the option of renewing the church from within. These individuals formed an association called *De Gereformeerde Bond* (= the Reformed Alliance) in 1906. In recent years there were still about three hundred congregations affiliated with the *Bond* or alliance, and it claimed no fewer than 400,000 members. The alliance was a sizable group within a much larger denomination (*De Hervormde Kerk* numbered 3,240,000 members in 1960) and was intended to be the conscience of *De Hervormde Kerk*. It has never been clear how much the established church has listened to this group within her borders. The alliance does not favor hymn singing but emphasizes the Psalms; it also stresses the necessity of personal conversion. It is almost a church within a church—an alliance that has exercised effective spiritual leadership for its supporters through traditional, confessionally sound preaching at every worship service.

With this historical background in mind, we are in a position to turn our attention to events in the Dutch Reformed churches in the twentieth century. Much of the church history touched on in the preceding pages serves as the essential backdrop for understanding events that would happen a little later. In a general way, the early part of the present century can be categorized as an advantageous time for the church. It had the opportunity to consolidate what it had received. Yet, at the same time, it was a period of marked worldliness and materialism. Holland was neutral during the World War I and profited materially as a result of her stand. Her cities were not ruined, her manpower was not decimated, and her commerce and industry could go on almost without interruption. Faced with the perennial problem of adapting the past to the needs of the present, the church was confronted with a challenge as it attempted to address the needs of the postwar period. She would have to give proper and effective leadership in the days to come.

Chapter 2
The Decade of the Twenties

Introduction

The decade of the 1920s began on a very somber note for the members of *De Gereformeerde Kerken*. The man who had been their leader and champion ecclesiastically and politically, Dr. Abraham Kuyper, died in the year 1920 at the ripe old age of eighty-two. Kuyper was a genius who had written a small library of books during his lifetime. He had the uncommon ability to write both scholarly works and meditations for the wider church membership. He had also edited two papers for many years. *De Heraut* (= the Herald) was a religious periodical for which he provided editorials, book reviews, and many kinds of articles. In this religious (not church) paper, long series of articles had flowed from his pen, and these were often later published in book form. Because the articles had been written in a popular form in the first place, the readership was well able to understand the books he published on the basis of them. Kuyper's books were read throughout the whole country, and they played a decisive role in forming a laity schooled in the finest Reformed theology of the day. The church membership read what theologians had to say.

His other paper was *De Standaard* (= the Standard), a daily paper, in which Kuyper set forth his theories on politics, education, economics, etc. He was the founder of a political party based on the Reformed view of life and called *De Antirevolutionaire Par-*

tij (= the Anti-revolutionary Party). Kuyper himself was elected to the second chamber of the national government where he represented the new Christian party. His work here along with his voluminous writing caused Queen Wilhelmina to appoint him Prime Minister in 1901. By the time of his death, he had given effective leadership to the Reformed people for forty years, and his influence would last far longer in the church he loved. His books were not only read, they were virtually devoured! His influence on the Dutch nation and churches can scarcely be measured. His works are still being quoted in Reformed circles around the world.

Another blow fell on the GKN in 1921 when another of her greatest leaders, Dr. Herman Bavinck, died. Kuyper and Bavinck certainly differed a great deal from each other, but each one made a deep impression on the church. Bavinck was not a natural leader like Kuyper, but he was *the* theologian. His four-volume work on Reformed dogmatics was a classic in which he systematized Reformed doctrine more precisely than had been done by his predecessors. No one knew the teachings of the fathers of the church more thoroughly than Bavinck did; moreover, he was a keen student of all the modern doctrinal publications as well.

Bavinck had begun his teaching career at the theological school at Kampen. When he left this school in 1902 and went to the Free University, a number of students followed him. His considerable scholarly reputation gave increased status to the Free University because the new professor of dogmatics attracted not only students from his own country but also from abroad. The Kampen school, however, had been deeply hurt by his departure, suffering loss both in numbers of students and in prestige. At the time, the Free University gave graduate degrees and Kampen was not allowed to do so because, as the specious argument of its opponents ran, it was a church school and the church could not give graduate degrees. They failed to recognize that it is the school, not the church, that confers degrees. Nevertheless, Kampen's theological school did survive Bavinck's departure, even though its student body was smaller as a result. Relations between the theological schools at Kampen and the Free University were strained by Bavinck's move. Tensions between the two schools must also be borne in mind in order to understand adequately some of the later difficulties experienced in the churches.

Kuyper had written a small library of books, and Bavinck, besides his dogmatics, wrote extensively on such subjects as Christian education and Christian psychology. But these two were not the only ones who were writing for the benefit of the Reformed churches. Holland was fortunate to have a publisher, J. H. Kok of Kampen, who was anxious to place good Reformed literature into the homes of the populace. This firm commissioned work on a set of commentaries that would cover all the books of the Bible and that would not be weighted down with any Hebrew or Greek words in the text of the commentary. (They were to go in the footnotes if they were considered necessary.) The members of the two theological faculties, Kampen and the Free University, were asked to contribute, as were a few other Reformed scholars in the Netherlands. An additional feature of the series was that a completely new translation was to be made of every book in the Bible.

The series of commentaries came to be known as *De Korte Verklaring* (= The Brief Explanation). Members of the churches could use the commentaries because they did not have material in Hebrew and Greek sprinkled throughout the text. It has proved to be a very usable tool for many devoted members of the churches. A large number of other works also flooded the book market during the decade of the twenties. The presence of a Reformed university in the Netherlands enabled a large number of able ministers to obtain advanced theological degrees. This, in turn, contributed to the welfare of the churches they served.

Although their two most prominent men in the GKN—Kuyper and Bavinck—had come to the end of their lives in the early 1920s and many were wondering who would assume the leadership of the denomination, these were also years of great profit for the churches. Major advances had been made in biblical scholarship, and as a result the church membership had been instructed better than ever before. Economically these were also good times for Holland, generally speaking. Neutrality during World War I, although the country favored Germany (after the war Kaiser Wilhelm was given sanctuary in Doorn, Holland, where he lived out the remainder of his days in opulence), had enabled Holland to do "business as usual" from the time the fighting stopped. The East Indies were still pouring their wealth into Holland. These economic conditions allowed the churches to pursue their work as in few previous decades. Missions flourished. Christian schools dotted the land. All these endeavors were enhanced by the better economic climate.

Although the church prospered outwardly and much had been done for the instruction of the people, there were certain warning signs. As has been mentioned before, it was also an age of worldliness. However, other problems of a far more serious nature were appearing, disputes that could shake the churches to their foundation. One problem of this kind is associated with the Rev. J. B. Netelenbos of Middelburg (GKN) who raised questions about the historicity of the first chapters of Genesis. In the view of many, he denied the infallibility of the Bible and also the Reformers' teaching that the Bible is perspicuous, that is, clear to all.

Netelenbos's theories about the first chapters of Genesis were part of a larger reinterpretation of the biblical text. It soon became evident that he not only considered Genesis 2 and 3 (the stories about Adam and Eve in the Garden of Eden) to be myths but he also held a similar opinion about the miracles of the Old Testament. The narratives about these, too, he regarded as mythological. His thinking on these points came to light in some of the sermons he preached. One of the members of his congregation, after hearing him voice opinions of these kinds, brought the matter to the church courts. It came to the synod of the GKN in 1920. There was no doubt within the denomination how the synod would rule on the matter. The authorities could hardly allow one of its ministers to attack the Scriptures, the very foundation on which the faith of the church rests. The synod of 1920 decided that there was no room in the offices of the church for someone who found mythological elements in the early chapters of Genesis and denied the factuality of biblical miracles. The Rev. Netelenbos was deposed from the ministry in the GKN. Later he joined *De Hervormde Kerk* where positions of the sort he had adopted were more readily acceptable.

It should be stressed that the GKN would not allow a place in the church in 1920 for the positions represented by Netelenbos. The synodical procedure was welcomed by the membership of the church. They felt that, if believers do not have a dependable, historically reliable Bible, they have nothing. The synod of 1920 left no doubt as to where it stood in regard to this question.

However, a short time later, a similar but far more ominous case came before the synod of the GKN. Dr. J. G. Geelkerken, a very popular minister of the GKN in Amsterdam, denied the historicity of the second and third chapters of Genesis. In this respect he agreed with Netelenbos who had just been deposed by the synod of 1920. It is surprising that cases so similar in character should follow so closely upon each other. Geelkerken's positions, which were developed in far greater detail than those of Netelenbos, were judged by the GKN synod of 1926 and found wanting. He, too, was deposed. The synod made it clear to everyone in the denomination that the first chapters of Genesis were to be recognized as being historical and not mythological. Thus, within the span of a half dozen years, two synods of the denomination had been called upon to deal with a similar or even the same problem.

It is strange that Geelkerken had learned nothing from the synod of 1920, which had condemned the position taken by Netelenbos, but advanced the same ideas once more. The more ominous aspect was that Geelkerken found so many supporters within the denomination. When he was deposed by the synod, he formed a new denomination called *De Gereformeerde Kerken in Hersteld Verband*. A few of the professors and about seventy students of the Free University joined the new denomination. It should be noted that Dr. S. Greijdanus, professor of New Testament at Kampen, voted against the deposition of Dr. Geelkerken at the 1926 synod, not because he had any sympathy for the views of Geelkerken (far from it), but because he did not believe that a synod had the right to depose a minister. As he understood church polity, deposition was the task of the local church council, which had responsibility for supervising the doctrine and conduct of the person who served the congregation as pastor. The stance adopted by Greijdanus is important to remember in order to understand the church polity debate of the 1940s.

The new denomination *De Gereformeede Kerken in Hersteld Verband* never played a significant role in the history of the Reformed churches in Holland. We may add as a postscript that in 1946 Dr. Geelkerken joined *De Hervormde Kerk*, and twenty-one years later (1967) the GKN rescinded the decision of 1926 to depose him. The fact that the denominational synod reversed a decision taken by one of its predecessors illustrates how much thinking in the GKN has changed within a span of forty years.

Klaas Schilder—the Early Years

The most important person in this study is Klaas Schilder. He played a highly significant role in the history of the Reformed churches of Holland from about 1920 until the day of his death in 1952. It is difficult to write about Schilder objectively, and it is not easy to avoid superlatives in describing his ability and accomplishments. Perhaps more was written about Schilder from 1920 to 1952 than about any other Dutch theologian. Whether the writers favored what he had to say or were strongly against it, everyone admitted that the man was brilliant. His was a life that was unique. People either loved him or hated him. He made either disciples or enemies. Many believe that he did more for the Reformed churches than any other person during his lifetime, while others are convinced that he brought schism into the church and sought his own glory. Whatever opinion people may have of him, he certainly cannot be ignored.

Although this is not a biography of Schilder, a few items of his early life may be necessary to relate so that it will be possible to understand the course of his adult life and his way of thinking more fully. He was born on December 19, 1890 in the city of Kampen. He was baptized within a congregation of *De Hervormde Kerk* to which his parents belonged at the time of his birth. His father died when the future theologian was only five years old. His widowed mother experienced trying times as she tried to support her family of several children as a widow; she had to take in laundry in order to make ends meet.

Schilder's early schooling was obtained in the grammar and high schools of Kampen. Not much is known about this particular period in his life, and it is also not especially pertinent to our purpose. He was a diligent student whose interests were tremendously broad. When he attended the Kampen theological school, his brilliance became immediately evident. His knowledge of the classical languages, Greek and Latin, became proverbial. Jan Waterink, a friend of his from their earliest days until the mid-1930s, remembered that while the other students were struggling with these languages, Schilder was writing poetry in them. He had a wonderful knowledge of literature. It was commonly admitted that he knew the German poet Goethe better than anyone of his time in the Netherlands. He was able to quote large parts of *Faust* from memory. He graduated from the theological school with highest honors in 1914.

Schilder served a total of six congregations during his ministry. It was not easy for his parishioners to follow him in his preaching. His voice was not at all clear, with the result that he had to do voice exercises all of his adult life. But it was especially the depth of his thinking that closed the doors for so many people who tried to understand him. A man in one of the last churches he served admitted that he, together with a group of others, had put forth extraordinary efforts to follow Schilder's train of thought because they were sure they would never have a minister like him again. Although his voice was not very clear, he was a very popular speaker. After only a couple years in the ministry, he received calls to the largest and most prestigious churches in the country. He was invited to speak for numerous gatherings on a wide variety of subjects.

Both in his preaching and in his lectures on diverse topics, he always showed that he was well prepared. No one had opened the Word of God to the people of that day as K. Schilder did. His knowledge of literature and philosophy staggered the imagination of both friend and foe.

Although Schilder kept a busy schedule as pastor of the churches he served, he somehow found time in the 1920s to write several books on a variety of subjects. For example, he wrote a series of meditations entitled *Licht in den Rook* (Light in the Smoke); *Tussen "Ja" en "Neen"* (Between Yea and Nay), a volume of essays on topics such as Satan, the naive Christian, mysticism, Calvin on the paradox of faith, and even psychoanalysis; and *De Openbaring van Johannes en het Sociale Leven* (The Revelation of John and Social Life). Later he would dismissively refer to these works as products of youth, but the books were solid in content.

In the latter part of the decade of the 1920s, the head of the J. H. Kok publishing house happened to read a meditation by a minister whose name, K. Schilder, was not familiar to him. Although unacquainted with Schilder, he was so intrigued by the content of the meditation on the sufferings of our Savior that he contacted Schilder and asked him to develop his thoughts on the passion into a book. Schilder accepted the offer and wrote his now famous trilogy on the sufferings of Christ. Dr. Henry Zylstra of

Calvin College in Grand Rapids, Michigan, translated these three volumes into English, and the Wm. B. Eerdmans Publishing Company issued them as *Christ in His Suffering, Christ on Trial*, and *Christ Crucified*. Through the trilogy the English-speaking world received its first taste of Schilder's writing.

Still today it is generally understood that no Reformed pulpiteer is able to preach adequately on the sufferings of our Lord without consulting Schilder's work. It was not only in the various Dutch Reformed communities that his treatment of the passion made its influence felt; it also found ready acceptance in other denominations. For example, the *Methodist Protestant Recorder* wrote about the first volume: "Now and then there comes from Europe a great book which forces itself upon the readers of this nation by the strength of its worth. This volume is such a book. Its study will mean a new day in the life of the preacher who digs into its rich mine of unusual thought" (quoted from the jacket of *Christ on Trial*).

In many ways there were similarities between A. Kuyper and K. Schilder. Both wrote extensively on a wide range of topics. Both were theologians of note. Both had their own idiosyncratic style. Both were able to write scholarly works as well as meditations for the general church membership. Schilder's vast knowledge of a number of disciplines besides theology made his writing scintillating. It has proved very difficult to translate his works because he almost wrote his own dictionary.

In addition to all the theological books that were published in Holland in the 1920s, there was also a large supply of religious papers issued to give church news and principal direction to the members. Virtually every *classis* or group of churches had its own *Kerkbode* (newsletter). These papers supplied their readership with the news of the area and also contained their own editorials or reprinted articles from other papers. There were several religious papers that had a national circulation. *De Heraut*, of which Dr. A. Kuyper was the longtime editor, has already been mentioned. After the death of Kuyper, his son, Dr. H. H. Kuyper, became the editor. The younger Kuyper was professor of church history and church polity at the Free University. *De Bazuin* (The Trumpet), while it did not become as well known in the United States as Dr. Kuyper's paper, also had considerable influence among the Reformed people in the Netherlands. Another paper—*De Wachter* (The Watchman)—had as its goal to further knowledge about and support of the theological school in Kampen.

Despite the presence of all these papers, some church members began to campaign after World War I for yet another national paper. Those who advocated a new publication wanted a paper that would speak especially to the youth of the church because they (at least according to some of their elders) could no longer grasp the content of the older papers. That is, they were eager to have the faith communicated to the young but realized that it would have to be presented in a different, more modern format. It is really not so surprising that there was agitation for an additional paper in the postwar period. Experience shows that changes are often desired after an upheaval (such as World War I) in the social and political life of a group.

A rather large committee was appointed to look into the matter of starting a paper for younger members of the church. The names of the men who served on the committee sound like a "Who's Who" of the ministers of the GKN of that day. They counted among them Dr. K. Dijk, Dr. H. C. De Moor, Dr. V. Hepp, Dr. B. Wielenga, Dr. H. Vande Vaart Smit, Dr. W. Buitendijk, and a few others. They were charged with the task of establishing a paper that would be true to the Reformed faith, that would be more progressive than the others (in this way addressing the interests of the young), and that would not fall into the more liberal camp but give positive direction to the church.

The committee met several times because it soon became evident that inaugurating a new paper is an enormous undertaking. Also the committee's work did not progress smoothly at all times.

After only a few meetings, Dr. De Moor indicated that he was not happy with the work of the secretary of the committee, Dr. H. Vande Vaart Smit. De Moor questioned his competence and also raised queries about how Reformed his positions were. Of course, no one could foresee at the time how much difficulty the GKN would have with Vande Vaart Smit twenty years later when he became an official of the Nazi government that ruled the Netherlands during World War II.

After much work had been done by the founding committee, the first issue of the new paper—*De Reformatie* (= The Reformation)—appeared in the fall of 1920. Dr. B. Wielenga had been named the editor, and he had the help of several very capable associates. K. Schilder was not among the men who launched the new venture. He did not yet belong to the "leading men" who started the paper because he was still a very young pastor (he had graduated from the theological school just six years before the first issue was published). However, he was deeply interested in the new publication and eagerly awaited developments. In its very first year, the paper carried a couple of articles by the Rev. K. Schilder.

De Reformatie was well accepted in the denomination although the number of subscriptions never was very large. Nevertheless, it soon had more subscriptions than some of the other national papers. One criticism of *De Reformatie* sprang up very soon: the paper did not offer as clear a direction as it was expected to do. The editorial staff did not unravel contemporary issues sharply enough in the estimation of many people and did not readily take a firm stand on debated points. The readership had anticipated a better product, something that would really distinguish *De Reformatie* from the many other papers. There was simply too much duplication. Dr. B. Wielenga was a capable man, but he was far too irenic in spirit to become involved in heated disputes. His temperament did not always serve him well in dealing with the issues of the day on which the readers of *De Reformatie* wanted guidance.

After approximately four years, Dr. Valentine Hepp was appointed editor in place of Wielenga. Hepp was a very capable theologian who knew the Reformed doctrines as well as anyone, and he was able to articulate them clearly. His was a rather strange style of writing—almost every sentence he penned was a new paragraph. He had not been editor very long before he was attacked by Prof. Buitendijk for not taking a clear and definite stand on a range of issues. As a result, two of the founders of *De Reformatie* were now at odds with each other. Not long after this, Buitendijk left the paper. He eventually left the GKN and affiliated with the Roman Catholic Church. Later several other objections were raised against the stands taken in *De Reformatie* in its early years.

Dr. V. Hepp had been appointed to the chair of dogmatics at the Free University in the mid-1920s. This was the chair formerly held by Dr. Herman Bavinck himself. It was not easy for Hepp to do justice to his work at the theological school and at the same time to the editorial work for *De Reformatie*. It was also in the mid-1920s that K. Schilder was appointed associate editor of the paper. With this appointment Schilder began an assignment that continued until the end of his life.

Many had learned to know and love him in the churches he served, but through his journalistic labors, the whole country became acquainted with him and could profit from his insights. The readership had to become used to his writing style, which differed from any they had seen before. He was often referred to as "the man who speaks in strange languages" although he was writing in the Dutch language. It was a challenge to read and understand Schilder. He played with the language. Similes and metaphors tumbled over each other. Foreign languages were no problem for him. Although he did not speak English, he read it fluently and he used German and French liberally. In one of his first articles for the paper, he repeatedly played with the words *veronderstelde wedergeboorte* (= assumed regeneration) to characterize the thinking of Rev. G. Wisse. It was humorous, and Dr. Hepp, the editor, warned the readers not to read the article in one sitting because their minds might play tricks on them. This was Schilder—a stylist with the heart of an artist.

In the late 1920s, a series of incidents caused relations between Hepp and Schilder to become strained. Hepp wrote a series of articles advocating a meeting of a Federation of Calvinists. His goal was to assemble Calvinists from around the world. The concept gained almost immediate support. The Reformed churches had never distinguished themselves by their zeal for such an ecumenical task, which was in fact their duty. Here was an opportunity to gather like-minded people from all countries and to meet together in order to strengthen one another and to discuss the problems of each group. Who would not be in favor of such a gathering? The press throughout the country took up the cause and enthusiastically supported it. So many were favorably inclined toward the proposal that a board was appointed to work out the details for an ecumenical assembly of Calvinists.

When Schilder saw the names of the men who were to serve on the planning board for the Federation, he was shocked to find the names of several who had followed Geelkerken out of the GKN in 1926 when the denomination had deposed him for his theories about the first chapters of Genesis. Although Schilder had to this point favored the concept of a Federation, he now opposed it because of the composition of the board. His argument was: How can we call men Calvinists when we declared three years ago that they were not Reformed? He considered these men neither Reformed nor Calvinists.

While the religious press had backed Dr. Hepp when he first advocated the Calvinist Federation, the clear and sharp criticisms of K. Schilder soon changed the minds of the majority of elders. Dr. F. Grosheide, one of Hepp's colleagues at the theological school of the Free University, argued in his support that the church should be able to speak of Calvinists "in a broader sense." His argument found few followers. Schilder's position was recognized by the vast majority as the only logical one. Schilder was now well known not only as a man with a sharp pen, but also as a very clear thinker. Hepp had made a trip to the United States in 1929—one of the years when the papers were full of arguments for and against the proposed Federation. Schilder was the acting editor-in-chief while Hepp was absent. Many have wondered about the propriety of an associate editor, acting editor-in-chief for the time, taking a strong position against the views of the permanent editor. Schilder had the same concern. He was highly sensitive to ethical matters and offered to resign. His offer was rejected by the publisher of the paper, Oosterbaan & Le Cointre of Goes.

To say the least, his writings in *De Reformatie* while Dr. Hepp was absent did not endear him to the editor. As a result of the whole unpleasant incident, Hepp resigned as editor of the paper. He felt that Schilder had undermined his influence. These two— Hepp and Schilder—were never on friendly terms again and their disagreements would become even sharper a few years later.

Schilder seized the opportunity he had as associate editor to write on a variety of topics. It soon became clear that he was a born journalist. He tackled the problems of the day and wrote at length on various doctrinal matters. For example, he penned lengthy articles on the church, common grace, and on contemporary cults. He had a profound respect for Dr. Abraham Kuyper and his writings; no one studied them more closely than Schilder. However, if he did not agree with the great Kuyper on certain points, he was not afraid to say so and always gave a well-reasoned account of his own stance. Here the mind of a genius was dealing with the writings of another genius. Only then do we honor Kuyper, said Schilder, when we correct him in those areas where he was wrong.

But he was touching Kuyper, the one man who, according to many, was not to be criticized. Kuyper's son, Dr. Prof. H. H. Kuyper, reacted angrily to anything written by Schilder that did not in every respect agree with his father's teaching. The one wrote in *De Reformatie* and the other in *De Heraut*, but the lines were being drawn. Schilder believed that Reformed theology would be calcified if one generation rigidly maintained the traditions of the previous one. He certainly did not dishonor Kuyper Sr., but he used his considerable ability to sit in judgment on the writings of Kuyper, especially his doctrine of the church, by the light of Scripture and confessions.

So, by the close of the 1920s, Schilder had become well known to the whole country through his paper. He had begun the decade as a little-known minister, but many recognized him as their champion ten years later. He had also made enemies of the two most powerful men in the GKN, Kuyper and Hepp. However, his star was rising. Through his journalistic endeavors, he enjoyed some of his greatest rewards and suffered some of his severest setbacks.

During the 1920s, both Schilder and Hepp had written extensively against the theology of Karl Barth which was making deep inroads in the state church. It was Schilder especially who saw where Barthianism would lead. He realized that, though the Barthians used terms such as election and reprobation and thus caused many to believe that theirs was only a different approach to the same Reformed theology, Barthian theology defined those shared terms very differently and that it would be fatal to everything the Reformed theologians had taught. He fought with the leaders in *De Hervormde Kerk*—the Drs. Haitjema, Van Niftrik, and Miskotte—who defended Barthian positions. They soon realized that they had an opponent who was master of his difficult subject.

Looking back over the 1920s, one must conclude that the foundations were laid both for several programs and for problems in the Dutch Reformed churches. The societies in the churches were standing on a solid foundation. Men and women as well as the youth of the church had excellent, up-to-date study materials. The churches continued to grow even though emigration to the

New World had removed many people from their rolls. But in especially significant ways, the 1920s laid the groundwork for the problems of later times. Attacks had been made on the historical reliability of parts of the Bible. The deviant theories of both Netelenbos and Geelkerken had been synodically condemned, but the same ideas and even far more radical ones were to be synodically approved in the same churches in the 1960s. The views propounded by these and later individuals did not change much over the years, but the attitude toward them was obviously quite different in the 1920s from what it was to be in the 1960s.

It had also been decided by the Board of the Free University during the 20s that it could no longer demand that its professors be members of *De Gereformeerde Kerken*. As a result, four members of its faculty were able to leave the GKN and join Geelkerken's group without placing their positions in jeopardy although the synod had declared the position of Geelkerken unreformed. This, too, did not bode well for the churches, because the historicity of the first chapters of Genesis was at stake. Forty years later the denomination allowed in her offices men who denied the historical character of the first eleven chapters of Genesis and even one who denied the atonement through the blood of Christ!

For Schilder the 1920s had indeed been the most turbulent time he had yet seen. How circumstances had changed for him! He had begun the decade as an obscure minister, but by its close, he had become the leader of a significant element in the churches. He had written prolifically. His books were very well received, and it usually did not take long after one of his books was published before a second edition was necessary. He had written extensively against the position of Dr. Geelkerken. He had begun his work on *De Reformatie* and would devote a large proportion of his efforts to the paper during the coming years. Lines had been drawn and positions had been taken. He would discover, however, that the turbulence of the twenties would not compare to the volatility of the thirties.

Chapter 3
The Decade of the Thirties

As has been mentioned before, Dr. Hepp resigned as editor of *De Reformatie* when Schilder, in Hepp's own paper, opposed what he had to say about the Federation of Calvinists. Schilder had offered to resign as an associate editor, and Hepp, too, had tendered his resignation. For his own reasons, the publisher did not accept the resignation of Schilder but did accept Dr. Hepp's offer. He wanted to keep Schilder and have a co-editorship of three men—Schilder, Dr. J. Waterink, and Dr. C. Tazelaar. The latter two were professors at the Free University, Tazelaar in literature and Waterink, although he was a theologian, in psychology. Dr. Hepp started his own paper, *Credo*, a short time later.

For Schilder the decade began in a highly auspicious manner. He had long cherished the hope that he would be able to do graduate study in theology and in this way to bring his academic training to an appropriate conclusion. Finances stood in the way of the pursuit of his goal. He was not born into a rich family, and his own family had grown. Consequently, he needed all he earned to support them. He had served a very large church in the city of Delft. He had been there a comparatively short time when he received a call from a church in the small town of Oegstgeest. No one thought he would accept the call, but he did. The reason: He was hoping that in a smaller church he would be able to find extra time for further study.

As it turned out, he did not gain more time for scholarship;

rather, he discovered that in a smaller church the meetings were as numerous as in a large church; there just were not as many people at them or at a worship service. His service at the church in Oegstgeest had been of short duration when he received a call to one of the largest churches in the country, Rotterdam Delfshaven. He accepted this call because he had given up on the idea of further study. He wrote to a personal friend, Rev. A. Boeienga, that he thought the remainder of his life would be taken up with "preaching, catechizing, and family visiting." He found joy in his work and had been doing it with great enthusiasm for sixteen years. He was an obedient child of his God. With the Apostle Paul, he could be satisfied in every state in which he found himself. But he was disappointed that the way to advanced study seemed to be closed.

However, Schilder did not realize that God's plans for his life were different from his. In the city of Rotterdam, he had a colleague, Rev. R. Zijlstra, who offered to loan Schilder the money needed to pursue a doctoral degree. The offer came as a pleasant surprise for Schilder. The consistory of the church then agreed to give him leave time for his project. The opportunity that he had strongly desired had now been given to him.

Once the possibility of pursuing an advanced degree had opened up for Schilder, he had to address the practical question of where would he continue his studies. Under normal conditions the answer would have been very simple: of course he would go to the Free University. But personal animosities and tensions had conspired to make the situation abnormal. He wished to study dogmatics, but he had crossed swords with the professor of dogmatics at the Free University, Dr. Hepp. In addition to the animosity between these two men, there were disagreements about theological points—something not unheard of in the history of the Christian Church. Because of these hard feelings and the ongoing principal debate between the two, Schilder did not feel that he could study under Hepp's tutelage. He sent a letter to the Free University outlining his reasons for not coming to the school. The letter is still in the files of the university and is very important because he was later accused of driving a wedge between Kampen and the Free University. The letter makes clear that this was not his intention at all. Instead of going to a Reformed university in his own country, he went to Erlangen, one of the older universities in Germany. Besides taking a leave of absence from his church, he also had to set aside his work as editor of *De Reformatie* during his period of study. He went to his scholastic work with great enthusiasm, and his diligence helped him accomplish much in a fairly short time.

Much of his study and his doctoral thesis dealt with the theology of Karl Barth. Schilder had done some writing on the Swiss theologian before, but he now delved into Barth's teaching more deeply. A. Kuyper had written his doctoral dissertation in Latin; Schilder wrote his in German.

His thesis was entitled *Zur Begriffsgeschichte des "Paradoxon"* (The History of the Concept of the "Paradox"). The idea of the paradox played a major role in the theology of Barth. For instance, Christ was the chosen one of God, but on the cross he was the reprobate. Schilder unraveled the whole theology of Barth and, in true Schilder fashion, made it clear that his theology was by no means Reformed in a traditional sense. Barth might speak of predestination, election, and reprobation, but he meant something quite different by them from what the classic Reformed thinkers had intended. His studies and his dissertation were considered so masterful that the University of Erlangen conferred on him a doctorate *summa cum laude*, with the highest honor, something this school had not given in one hundred years! A student of Schilder's caliber was an honor for any school, of course, and it is sad that the Free University could not share in his achievement.

Schilder was in Erlangen from 1930 to 1933. While he was there, he saw the rise of National Socialism and gained a firsthand understanding of the philosophy that drove the movement. His eyewitness knowledge of Naziism enabled him to give informed leadership in the Dutch churches and in his own country ten years later. It is regrettable that Dutch leaders did not listen to him when he spoke and wrote about National Socialism later in the 1930s.

When Schilder returned to Holland, he resumed both his former roles eagerly. He had submitted a few articles to *De Reformatie* during his years in Germany, but during his studies, he was unable to make regular contributions as he had done previously. Never was there a word in *De Reformatie* as to his progress toward the goal of his study. It was Schilder's unbending policy that items of a personal nature were to be kept out of the paper. Dr. Waterink did, however, mention in his own column that Schilder had obtained his degree and the way he had obtained it. A few years later, when he had been in the ministry for twenty-five years, some of the other writers for *De Reformatie* "plotted" with the publisher to place something in the paper about the anniversary.

Schilder felt somewhat embarrassed when someone would write about him in a forum so public as *De Reformatie*. He firmly believed that the space should be used for more important matters. So much was this the case that when one of the regular contributors to *De Reformatie* had published a book, the author had to review it himself so that it did not appear as if the paper were promoting any individual's work. He was also glad to return to the congregation in Rotterdam. He had done much for the congregation, but they had done much for him too. True to his character, he was very quickly back in full stride. He did everything with almost reckless abandon. He was not easy on himself. The number of hours Schilder put in every week was staggering. He used every moment of the day. There are so many anecdotes about his method and work ethic. He wrote, of course, in his own study but also in trains and in the homes of families with whom he might spend a night while traveling. Once while standing in the aisle of a full train, he is supposed to have asked the man standing in front of him whether he could use his back as a desk for writing.

He usually managed to submit his voluminous pages of *hand-*

written material just before the deadline at the publishing house. Almost no one could read his terrible penmanship. Someone even wrote a poem to praise the one poor printer at Oosterbaan's who was able to decipher Schilder's script—something he did with difficulty. Some of his material was written on standard-sized paper, other parts were written on small pieces of paper, and some of it on pieces of cardboard. He was always so pleased when he would get the finished printed copy of *De Reformatie* in his hands. It was almost miraculous that a fine finished product emerged from the chaos he had brought to the publisher.

Professor at Kampen

As previously noted, when Dr. Herman Bavinck left Kampen in 1902 to go to the Free University, the school at Kampen suffered a very serious blow. Bavinck had been the drawing card for foreign students as well as for many from his own country. Several students followed him from Kampen to Amsterdam. What would the Kampen school do now? A man such as Bavinck could not be replaced. Some suggested that the best course would be to merge the Kampen theological school with the theological school of the Free University. However, a merger of this kind was simply unacceptable to a large number of people. They (many of them readers of *De Wachter*) had a dogged determination to continue their own school, which had its historical roots in the Secession of 1834.

The student body at Kampen was considerably smaller after the departure of Bavinck. The church searched for someone to take his place and gave the nod to Dr. A. G. Honig, who taught at Kampen for about thirty years. Dr. Honig did not have a major impact even though he gave solid instruction to his students during all the time he taught dogmatics at Kampen. Honig used Bavinck's dogmatics as the textbook for his classes and added nothing to what Bavinck had written other than a "Handbook." In his opinion, Bavinck had uttered the last word in Reformed dogmatics, and a "Handbook" was sufficient to cover the subject after Bavinck's definitive pronouncements.

In 1933 Dr. Honig reached retirement age. Where would the church now turn for a successor? In the opinion of the board of the school, the ministers of the day, and the lay members of the church, K. Schilder, who had now earned his doctorate, had to receive serious consideration. The GKN synod meeting in 1933 shared that opinion. Schilder was elected to the chair of dogmatics and ethics by unanimous vote. If ever there was a "natural" for such a position, it was Schilder. His academic training left nothing to be desired. He had given evidence of being able to write scholarly works and also works that met the needs of the general reader. He was well known in the churches and had their confidence. Everyone knew where he stood because it was against his whole nature to hide his opinions. His positions were very positive. There was no fence-straddling by Schilder.

It was widely believed that his abilities ought to benefit all the churches, not only the single congregation he happened to serve. He had been in the ministry of the church for nineteen years and was therefore not only acquainted with theology but also the needs of the average parishioner. The membership of the churches looked for many years of good leadership from Schilder, who had made such a deep impression on so many people. Could something of the aura of the Bavinck years return to Kampen? Would this school, through the brilliant work of its new professor, draw foreign students again? The church was more than satisfied with the appointment the synod had made, and Schilder was delighted with the opportunity to be of even greater service to his God and to the churches than he had been in the past.

He was installed as professor at Kampen early in 1934. As is customary in the GKN, he became emeritus minister of the church he had been serving, the congregation at Rotterdam Delfshaven.

The procedure in the GKN differs from the one followed by Reformed churches in North America. Under the Dutch system, a minister keeps all the prerogatives of the ministry and remains under the spiritual care of the church of which he is an emeritus pastor. Retirement, sickness, or broader service in the churches is reason enough for a *classis* to grant emeritation.

Schilder usually referred to himself by his initials (K. S.) in *De Reformatie*, and from now on, we will also refer to him in this way. He threw himself into his new work with great enthusiasm. He was in his element. Now he could devote himself to serious study as never before. He was soon known as a superb teacher who had the love of his students and was concerned about their welfare. He was well aware of the new responsibility placed on him, i.e., the training of the future ministers of the churches. He gladly shouldered the burden and also retained the editorship of *De Reformatie*. His double duties made for a heavy workload, but he had grown accustomed to a busy life.

It seemed as though a new day had dawned for both the Kampen theological school and for K. S. It seemed at first that beautiful years lay ahead for both. But the early promise was quickly overtaken by residual problems from the 1920s. Soon after Schilder had been installed as professor of dogmatics at Kampen, the professor of dogmatics at the Free University, Dr. V. Hepp, began to hold classes secretly (that is, they were not announced in the school's catalogue) in the university building in which he attacked the views of K. S. on the doctrine of the church. Hepp adhered to the Kuyperian understanding of the church as "pluriform," that is, the one true church manifested itself in many denominations and groups. Schilder took a somewhat different approach and emphasized the oneness of the church in the sense that there could be only one true church in any area and that one church was to be considered the body of Christ.

Both students and ministers were invited to attend Hepp's classes, although the classes were not advertised in the normal way.

Not surprisingly, it proved difficult to maintain the secrecy of these classes, and the matter was soon brought to the attention of Schilder himself. K. S. considered what Hepp was doing to be thoroughly unchristian and dangerous to the welfare of the churches. Hepp characterized those who held to Schilder's position as *epigonen*, i.e., that of individuals who lacked the ability to formulate original thoughts and simply parrot the views of others. His opposition to his colleagues at Kampen had taken a decidedly unpleasant turn. Naturally K. S. took up the controversy on the pages of *De Reformatie*.

A long and bitter polemic resulted. Schilder would not allow what Hepp was doing to pass without all the churches being fully aware of what was happening. On a very practical basis, he argued, he should have been invited to Hepp's classes because, as emeritus minister of Rotterdam Delfshaven, he was an area minister, and they were the ones who had been invited to attend. More basically, he knew that some of his students might go to the Free University for graduate study and did not wish to have his teaching negated by Dr. Hepp. Hepp, however, ignored what K. S. was writing and went on as though what he was doing was perfectly acceptable behavior. Hepp naturally found no backing for his position in the Reformed press. Both ministers and laymen condemned what he was doing.

Since neither of the protagonists was about to concede the point, the debate became sharp and prolonged. Some members of the churches dismissed the whole affair as only a difference of opinion among learned men. K. S. quickly rejected this idea. The whole church had a stake in such matters, he argued, and the issue should therefore be aired before the entire denomination. Finally one of the "leading men" (some think it was Dr. Colijn) asked both Hepp and Schilder to quit writing on the subject because he believed the dispute would hurt the churches. Hepp agreed immediately, and K. S. wrote that he would stop for the present but would take the subject up again if circumstances warranted it.

Again in the church's history, the lines were drawn sharply; clear positions had been taken. It was Hepp versus Schilder and therefore almost necessarily Amsterdam versus Kampen. The dispute arising from sharp differences between the two men did not bode well. Who knows to what degree envy and personal animosity were involved in these differences? Amsterdam and its dogmatician had received the accolades in the past, but a fresh wind was blowing through the churches and the new professor of dogmatics at Kampen was becoming very popular in both academic and ecclesiastical circles. The fact that Hepp and Schilder were not able to work together for the glory of the name of their God and for the welfare of the churches would soon produce regrettable results.

Even though the Calvinistic Federation that Dr. Hepp had proposed a few years earlier had been rejected in Holland, he now began to write in his new paper, *Credo*, about a "Calvinistic Congress." As the name suggests, it differed very little from his previously defeated proposal. Nevertheless, a board was appointed to implement the ideas presented by Dr. Hepp. It so happened that this board too was comprised in part of men who had followed the teachings of Dr. Geelkerken—the minister deposed by the synod of 1926. Schilder advanced the same argument against the second board as he had against the first: How can men whose beliefs about the first chapters of Genesis were declared unreformed in 1926 be the leaders in a Calvinistic Congress? Because of the composition of the board for the Calvinistic Congress, he opposed it as he had the Calvinist Federation.

However, on this occasion a new element came to his attention. Among the names of the men who were to form the board was that of Dr. J. Waterink, who had stood shoulder to shoulder with Schilder at an earlier time. Schilder wrote that inclusion of his name must be a printing error. But it was not a mistake. Dr. Waterink, who had been a close personal friend of K. S. since their early days in school and was co-editor with him of *De Reformatie*, had in this instance rejected the position of K. S. and had gone to the side of those who favored a "broad" board. K. S. considered this the work of a traitor.

The publisher of the paper now called in all three editors, Schilder, Waterink, and Tazelaar. He concluded that the time had come for the paper to be in the hands of one editor. He accepted the resignations of both Waterink and Tazelaar because he had made it plain to them that he wanted Schilder as editor. So another change in the leadership of the paper took place. Some even called these changes "Palace Revolutions." Under the sole editorship of K. S., *De Reformatie* would calmly go its own way and continue the emphasis of the past.

Waterink and Tazelaar began a new paper called *Calvinistische Weekblad* (= Calvinist Weekly). They stated that it was their intention to allow no polemics in their paper. K. S. reminded them of the dispute Waterink had carried on against a certain Rev. Steen when he was still writing in Schilder's paper. Waterink's polemics too had been very sharp. According to K. S., the worst polemic was to say that there will be no place for polemics in your paper.

De Reformatie was now under one unified leadership. Not only did K. S. write the editorials, he also edited *Persschouw*, i.e., a review of the press. In these columns he let his gaze run over what had been written in other papers. It seemed as though he had read everything that was published. Many a *Kerkbode* editor was surprised to see his words appearing in *De Reformatie*. K. S. would usually give his own comments on what he quoted from others. He not only engaged in controversies with Dr. Hepp but also with many others. He wrote a long series of articles against the position of Dr. O. Noordmans of *De Hervormde Kerk* on the subject of common grace. He wrote many articles on *De Pluriformiteit der Kerk*, a difficult concept to translate because there is no adequate English equivalent for *Pluriformiteit*. Suffice it to say that he differed in his view of the church from both A. Kuyper and V. Hepp. In Schilder's view the name *church* may not be given to all that calls itself *church*. Christ has only one body. Some of K. S.'s followers may have gone too far with this concept, but in his own writing, his meaning is clear. He again emphasized for church members the teachings of the Articles 27–29 of the Belgic Confession, especially about the contrast between the true and false church. One of the major contributions that K. S. made to Dutch Reformed thinking was in the area of ecclesiology—a subject that has important consequences for one's understanding of worship and the offices in the church. K. S. enriched Reformed theology with his understanding of and emphasis on the doctrine of the church.

He also wrote many articles on the idea of the covenant and on the matter of "Promotie Recht," i.e., the right of Kampen as well as the Free University to offer advanced degrees. This topic always aroused strong feelings on the two sides. Some thought that the synod of 1920 had forbidden anyone to broach the subject again in the churches. Schilder did not agree. He believed that, even though the Kampen theological school was the school of the churches, it should have the same rights as her sister institution in Amsterdam because it was the school, not the church, which bestowed degrees. His position was opposed by both Hepp and Dr. H. H. Kuyper. K. S. also wrote numerous articles about practical problems in the churches. To some it seemed as though there was no theological or ecclesiastical problem on which he did not comment.

The Debates of the Thirties

Several references have already been made to the fact that K. S. was without a doubt a polemicist—a fighter for the positions he held. He believed that if someone decided to write about the controversial matters of the time, he would have a hard time avoiding battles of the pen. Therefore when Waterink and Tazelaar promised that there would be no polemics in their new paper, Schilder considered that the worst kind of polemics. He was not afraid to tackle the most difficult and involved issues of the day. He feared no man or issue! He was, of course, not the only controversialist of the time. In fact, it seemed as though every paper and every editor engaged in this form of writing in the 1930s.

The methods used by the various polemicists of the 1930s have given rise to extended discussion. Some of the writers were relatively mild in their approach, while others were far more aggressive. K. S. has been accused of being the sharpest polemicist of the decade, and very likely the charge is true. He also kept at it more tenaciously than any other editor of the time. He did not drop a matter until the subject was exhausted. Everyone stood amazed at his erudition. He poured out enormous quantities of biblical and confessional proof for any position he defended. His knowledge of the fathers and the modern theologians and of literary sources overwhelmed those who tried to debate with him. He was sharp. Was he too sharp?

In comparison with late twentieth-century writing in church papers, he certainly seems to have been overly cutting and aggressive. However, he really did not attack individuals; he was far more interested in the issues. For nearly all who met him, his personality did not at all fit the image of an accomplished warrior of the printed page. He was strongly democratic and loving in his personal relationships. He could talk to the uneducated as well as to the learned. But he insisted that principles had to be true and clear; otherwise they would have to be corrected and clarified. The Reformers had also been very sharp in their disputes. Yet, Schilder was at times too polemical. He made some unnecessary enemies, and he, like others, seemed incapable of dropping a debated point before it had been exhausted. He, too, was a sinner, saved by the grace of God. Many of the difficulties of the 1930s came about because of either improper ways of disagreeing or words that were unnecessarily harsh.

In fairness, it should also be stated clearly that K. S. always quoted his opponents completely, no matter how boring he might sometimes find this to be. For example, when he was carrying on a debate about common grace with Dr. O. Noordmans, he filled page after page of the valuable space in *De Reformatie* quoting Noordmans. No reader, therefore, received a one-sided report from his writing. The readers knew what the point of the dispute was. The other controversialists did not always take the same balanced course.

K. S., however, had offended a number of individuals and especially some leaders of the GKN. Many of them would never forgive him for what he was doing. They considered him a troublemaker. Hepp, who had begun his career as professor of dogmatics with such high expectations but whose reputation seemed now to be eclipsed by K. S., tried to rescue his own position and that of the Free University in his writings against Schilder. Dr. H. H. Kuyper at one time pleaded his own advanced age as being reason enough for an opponent to deal gently with him and in this way attempted to avoid wading into the controversies of the day.

But issues were Schilder's concern. He was insistent that the membership of the churches had to be informed about dangers such as the inroads of Barthianism and the weakening of the doctrines of the church and covenant, which were threatening their welfare. In the face of such dangers, he believed, a responsible theologian could not express himself through honeyed speech or writing. Surely there was no lack of interest in the churches in the 1930s about the problems being debated. One could soon discover, when speaking to a fellow church member, which paper he read. K. S. gave leadership and did not care to give a "warmed over" version of past problems or of antiquated ideas.

By means of both his teaching at the Kampen theological school and his writing in *De Reformatie*, he exerted a deep influence on a large number of younger ministers. They found his ideas stimulating. In particular, his emphasis on preaching and his way of expounding the text of Scripture deeply impressed them as being unique. He emphasized "redemptive historical" preaching. That is, he stressed that all of the Bible is focused on Christ and that every text must be approached from its location within the history of revelation. With this type of preaching, of which Schilder was a master, the minister in the pulpit would do justice to the text and to its place in the long process of revelation. As a result of Schilder's emphasis on these matters, preaching was rejuvenated in many of the churches. The local pastor probably was not able to proclaim the message in so masterful a way as K. S., but at least Schilder had given him a fresh approach. These younger ministers eagerly awaited the publication of *De Reformatie* every week. Nevertheless, K. S. was maligned by many others who did not like his method of writing and disapproved of his tone.

The Synod of 1936 and Its Effects

The synod of the GKN meets every three years. It had met in 1933 and appointed K. S. professor of ethics and dogmatics at the Kampen theological school. The next synod met in 1936, with nothing on its agenda to arouse any concerns. It looked as though this would be an ecclesiastical assembly that dealt mostly with routine matters. But the rules of order for the synod are different in the GKN from those in North America. In the synods of the Reformed churches in North America, nothing may be brought to the floor of synod that has not passed the scrutiny of minor assemblies or of committees or boards previously appointed by synod. But in the Dutch synods, it is permissible, it seems, to bring to the floor of synod matters that had not been considered in any minor assembly. In the middle of the proceedings at the 1936 synod, two of the delegates brought up the matter of the harsh controversies that were being conducted in the religious press and bemoaned the acrimonious tone of the disputes.

Some prominent individuals, Dr. H. H. Kuyper especially, expressed their joy that the issue was coming before the synod. Schilder spoke, addressing the point because he realized that it was mainly aimed at him. He defended the practice of polemics on the grounds that it contributed to a healthy church life and did not wish to have all disputes judged merely by their tone. As he put it, one should study the substance of what had been written; people would then understand that the church had made giant strides forward in recent years.

Dr. Kuyper countered that the situation in the churches was desperate, occasioned by the bitter fighting that was current in the press. As he saw them, the conditions in the churches were worse than in the days prior to Assen, i.e., the Synod of Assen, which had condemned the position of Dr. Geelkerken in 1926. At that time there had also been great unrest in the churches, and the decision of the Assen Synod had caused some ministers, Geelkerken in the lead, and a number of other members to leave the GKN and to form a small denomination of their own.

Kuyper had also participated in his share of controversies during the last few years but in a different way. He and Dr. Hepp had written against various positions enunciated by K. S. They, however, produced neither proof from Scripture and the confessions nor what Schilder considered convincing argumentation. Their procedure stood in sharp contrast to Schilder's method. True, he wrote harshly, sometimes even caustically, but what others had written on a subject was quoted fully and his own arguments could be judged by any reader. Both Schilder and the aging Prof. Dr. S. Greijdanus argued their point at the synod but to no avail. The synod of 1936 passed a motion that the vicious disputes carried on in the press during the last few years be stopped. The proposal had come to the synod under the heading of "differences of opinion"; however, the motion that was adopted contained the expression "doctrinal differences." The substitution of *doctrine* for *opinion* involved a noteworthy change that seemed unwarranted by the evidence that was adduced.

K. S. was profoundly disturbed by the manner in which the synod had conducted its business and by the final decisions it made. A "blue ribbon" committee was appointed by the GKN synod of 1936 to study the "doctrinal differences" it had uncovered and bring its report to the following synod that would meet in 1939. Both Hepp and Schilder were elected as members of the committee as well as such men as Prof. Greijdanus, Dr. J. Vollenhoven (professor of philosophy at the Free University), and Dr. G. Aalders (professor of Old Testament at the same institution). Two prominent ministers were added to the committee: Dr. J. Thijs and Rev. J. Schouten. K. S. termed the day when the synod had made its decision "that dark Thursday." Although it had adopted for all practical purposes the views of Dr. Kuyper, K. S. thought following the synod that the results would not be very serious because of the personnel of the committee chosen to deal with the disagreement about how controversies were to be handled in the religious press. He was badly mistaken.

Only a short time after the meeting of the 1936 synod, Dr. Hepp published a series of brochures under the title *Dreigende Deformatie* (= threatening deformation). In them he discussed some of the more important doctrines that were then at issue. Eventually there were to be six of the pamphlets. In the brochures he neither named the individuals nor the works he was citing. He considered his anonymous approach to be the best method for arriving at the desired results, namely, to be of service to the churches. Only four of the promised six brochures were ever published. It proved difficult to combat the ideas he propounded because it was not always clear whom he was attacking or where to find the material he quoted or used. Yet discerning readers soon realized that he was writing against some of the teachings of K. S.

A little while later, it also became evident that he was writing against the views of H. Dooyeweerd and Vollenhoven (two professors at the Free University who had concentrated their efforts on developing a Christian philosophy), but they, too, found it difficult to defend themselves against Hepp's kinds of assaults. It did not take long before the whole religious press was angered by what Hepp was doing. Naturally, K. S. was not silent, but he found it frustrating to reply.

Dr. Hepp's brochures with their peculiar style also made it virtually impossible for the synodical committee to do its work, since one committee member (Hepp) had attacked at least two others anonymously (Schilder and Vollenhoven). How could the committee work toward an objective view of the facts in the area of their mandate when one member had already condemned what other members thought? Kuyper felt that what Hepp was doing was proper, but very few others agreed.

It did not take long before Prof. Greijdanus informed the chairman of the committee, Rev. Schouten, that he could no longer remain a member. The whole atmosphere created by Hepp was foreign to the heart and soul of Greijdanus. Some time later Schilder and Vollenhoven, under these curious circumstances, began to meet by themselves although they did not actually resign from the committee, as many have claimed. The work of the committee had been made much more difficult by the underhanded and unethical methods of one member. The group struggled along without the input of Greijdanus, Vollenhoven, and K. S., three of its most able members.

So, while the synod had hoped to end the bitterness that had become so prominent in the church papers, the battles resumed soon after the synod adjourned in 1936. The result was hardly unexpected. It proved too difficult for writers who were accustomed to forceful debates in print to remain silent while a professor at the Free University was publishing brochures attacking anyone and everyone in scatter-gun fashion.

At the same time, K. S. published in *De Reformatie* two "Open Letters" to Dr. H. H. Kuyper in which he answered many of the allegations Kuyper had made against him. He also tried to reason with Kuyper about his conduct and words during the last synod. For a long time, there was no answer. Finally Kuyper answered, also by means of an "Open Letter" in *De Heraut*. He retracted virtually none of the allegations he had made against K. S. in the past. He spoke of the pain K. S. had caused him through his writings. He also offered some "fatherly advice" to his younger colleague. Schilder did not appreciate Kuyper's reply because he had left everything as it was before and had not touched on the issues at stake. He had expected more. Schilder and Kuyper had met at the synod to clear up any personal problems Kuyper might have had with him. Schilder interpreted their time together as a conciliatory meeting, but Kuyper saw it differently and wrote of their "so-called reconciliation" at the synod. K. S., who always emphasized the words of Scripture—"Let your yea be yea, and your nay nay"—could not understand Kuyper's reaction.

Although polemical journalism was perhaps the most important subject addressed by the synod of 1936, there were also a few other issues that were significant and turned out far more favorably for Schilder. He had written and spoken in many places about the evil philosophy of Naziism. The National-Socialist theory of government and its relation to the people had its foundations in the philosophies of Hegel and Nietzsche. Holland counted a sizable number of Nazis among its citizens; they were organized as the NSB, the National Socialist Alliance.

Schilder had been in Germany studying for his doctoral degree when Hitler's fanatical group was coming into its ascendancy. K. S. concluded that it was totally inconsistent to be a member of this National Socialistic Party and of the church of Christ at the same time. He spoke on this issue throughout the Netherlands and warned against the danger Naziism posed to the nation and to the churches. He unmasked Dr. H. M. Vande Vaart Smit, who had been present at the birth of *De Reformatie*, as the GKN minister who was now in charge of the German religious news service in Holland. In other words, Vande Vaart Smit was in the employ of the Nazis. There were frequent denials on the part of the accused, but these were unsuccessful because K. S. adduced incontrovertible proof of his involvement with the Germans. Many members of the GKN and a large number of its leaders could not imagine that Schilder's charges could be true. Later it was decisively shown that Schilder had been right about Vande Vaart Smit from the beginning.

K. S. believed that the GKN synod should take a firm stand against the NSB and urge the consistories to discipline members who also belonged to the National-Socialist party. The synod of 1936 agreed. There could be no place in the GKN for those who adhered to Naziism.

At the same time, there were student organizations that were leaning toward communism. Some of the student members of the GKN were also on the lists of these groups. The GKN synod decided that consistories should deal with these students in a disciplinary manner. So, as far as K. S. was concerned, the decisions of the synod of 1936 were not entirely disappointing.

At nearly the same time, a seemingly minor event occurred. A student named M. Bouwman who had studied under H. H. Kuyper at the Free University wrote a doctoral thesis in which he advocated an interpretation of the church order that was foreign to traditional Reformed church polity. In his view, a *classis* (a regional group of churches or their representatives) is *higher* in authority than a consistory, or church governing board, and a synod is the *highest* ecclesiastical body in authority.

Kuyper, by accepting the dissertation, placed his approval on Bouwman's interpretation. But the dissertation and its implications did not escape the notice of Prof. S. Greijdanus, also an expert on church polity. He saw clearly the consequences of Bouwman's theory. In the first place, it denied the whole system of church polity as taught by A. Kuyper. Second, it would allow a synod to discipline a consistory and suspend or depose its mem-

50

bers. Only the local consistory, together with a neighboring consistory, had the right and the power to suspend office bearers, according to Greijdanus. Later the church polity defended by Bouwman and accepted by H. H. Kuyper would be used by the GKN against K. S., Greijdanus, and many others.

In the late 1930s, Schilder took on a new project. He certainly was busy enough with the two positions he already held, but for a long time, he had been thinking of writing his own dogmatics. He was not interested in writing another tome like that of H. Bavinck, but he also felt that it would not suffice to write only a handbook as his immediate predecessor, Honig, had done. K. S. hit on a novel approach to presenting his own ideas on Reformed dogmatics and for dealing with the problems of contemporary as well as historic Reformed theology. He, with the concurrence of his publisher, decided to write a commentary on the Heidelberg Catechism. They agreed that in order to reach as many people as possible, it would be wise to place a copy of each segment of his dogmatics in *De Reformatie*. K. S. was able to cover only ten of the fifty-two Lord's Days in the catechism before he died. His commentary did far more than simply take its place alongside many others; it was totally different from all the commentaries on the market at that time. When we remember the topic of his doctoral thesis, it comes as no surprise to learn that his treatment of the catechism includes an in-depth study of Barth's theology. K. S. had intended for his commentary to have the practical result of helping ministers as they prepared sermons on the catechism; in this regard, however, his success proved quite limited. His dogmatic commentary is essentially a work that explains the catechism through demanding theological analysis.

In the period we are studying, a number of Dutch theologians, professors from both the Free University and Kampen, had received invitations to visit Reformed churches in the United States. When they reached the United States, they would usually travel extensively and instruct members of the Reformed churches through preaching and teaching. Dr. Abraham Kuyper had come to America not only to meet with the people who were directly related to the GKN, but also to give the Stone Lectures at Princeton. Bavinck did the same a few years later. In 1929 Dr. Hepp had been in the United States and had been very cordially received. Greijdanus and Prof. H. Bouwman (not the author of the dissertation mentioned above) had also visited the United States, and later many others would come. It was always a delight for the membership of the Reformed churches, a large percentage of whom had been born in the Netherlands and were still able to understand the Dutch language, to listen to the scholars from Holland.

In 1938 K. S. received an invitation to travel to the United States. He had often expressed a desire to make such a visit, and it pleased him very much to receive an invitation to come. A committee had been formed in the U.S., not only to invite him, but also to arrange a very busy schedule of preaching and lecturing. K. S. considered this to be a great honor. However, it seemed as though there would always be some difficulties attending even his best moments. Rev. H. J. Kuiper, the editor of *The Banner*, the official magazine of the Christian Reformed Church (CRC), wrote in his column that he thought it would be far better if K. S. would not come at this time. He feared that Schilder might bring the theological differences that were being debated in Holland to the United States—especially his position on common grace or the idea that God extends certain kinds of favor to both the elect and the non-elect.

Differences about common grace had stirred up heated controversies in the CRC in the early 1920s, eventually leading to a denominational split in 1924 when the Revs. H. Hoeksema, H. Danhof, and G. OpHof were deposed by the CRC for denying that there was such a thing as common grace. It was well known that Schilder's understanding of common grace differed from the position taken by the synod of the CRC in 1924. The editor of *The Banner* feared that the wounds caused in 1924, now somewhat healed after the passage of fourteen years, would be reopened.

Perhaps *The Banner* editorial would have done little damage if it had been confined to the readers of its American audience. However, Dr. H. H. Kuyper immediately printed the editorial in his paper, *De Heraut*. Because most of the readers of the Dutch paper were not able to read English, Kuyper aided them with a somewhat slanted translation of the piece. For example, when H. J. Kuiper had called K. S. a "warrior for the faith," Kuyper rendered the phrase as "fighter for the faith." As a consequence of Kuyper's reprinting the article, a disagreement within the CRC spilled over into the Netherlands. Thus, the honor bestowed on K. S. by the invitation to America was not appreciated by some Reformed members in the United States and subsequently in the Netherlands. There clearly were people who would rather not have seen him carry out the visit. Nothing like this had ever happened before to one of the Dutch theologians. Schilder felt the rejection acutely. He knew H. H. Kuyper well, but he was surprised that he would stoop to hurting him by reprinting an editorial meant for an audience in another country. He answered Kuyper in his own paper and pointed out the unethical, to say nothing of the unfriendly, way in which Kuyper had brought this editorial to the attention of the reading public in Holland. In the end, despite all the controversy, he accepted the invitation to visit the United States because he had also received a flood of positive letters from CRC members.

K. S. arrived on the east coast of the United States in the fall of 1938 and was royally welcomed by both the ministers and members of the Christian Reformed Church in the East. In particular, the articles written by Rev. E. Van Halsema in *De Wachter*, a Dutch-language paper of the CRC, especially, made it clear to the whole denomination that the editor of *The Banner* had blundered badly in urging Schilder not to come. Van Halsema, with his poetic way of writing, showed what a delight it had been to hear K. S. in sermons and lectures. In his judgment, there was no need to fear that Schilder would bring any theological or ecclesiastical difficulty to the CRC. The eastern churches in the U.S. found K. S. to be thoroughly Reformed and a pleasant person besides.

As he spoke, he provided fresh insights into problems and issues facing the churches. Schilder's schedule was more than full, but he managed to keep all the appointments that had been made for him. Enormous crowds came to hear the famous Dutch theologian even though he always spoke in the Dutch language. Many had become acquainted with his thinking through reading his magisterial trilogy on the sufferings of Christ. Many others were readers of *De Reformatie*. It can honestly be said that he took the East by storm. He was in that area throughout the holiday season of 1938.

While he was in the eastern part of the country, he seized the opportunity to visit with Dr. C. Van Til of Westminster Theological Seminary (a longtime correspondent for *De Reformatie*) as well as with the elderly Dr. Geerhardus Vos, who had been a faculty member at Calvin Theological Seminary and later at Princeton Theological Seminary. He took great pleasure in these contacts with theologians of like mind. He could speak with them about the newest problems in Reformed theology as well as about the philosophical differences one met in so many places.

In January 1939 K. S. arrived in Grand Rapids, Michigan, the center of the CRC activity and the city in which *The Banner* was published and where its editor lived. It was announced in the Grand Rapids *Press* that Dr. Prof. K. Schilder would preach at the Eastern Avenue Christian Reformed Church in Grand Rapids on the following Sunday. The service was scheduled to begin at 2:00 P.M. The author was present on this occasion and can therefore provide an eyewitness account. Before 1:00 P.M., there were no empty seats left in the large sanctuary. Those who came later had to sit on folding chairs in the aisles, on the steps to the balconies, or on the steps of the pulpit.

The pastor of the Eastern Avenue Church, Rev. W. P. Van

Wyk, introduced K. S. In his own inimitable way, he drew attention to the fact that there were usually only forty to fifty present for the afternoon Dutch service—and now this overflowing crowd. The people had come to hear a master theologian and preacher. To say that the air was heavy with anticipation is putting it mildly. The singing of the first Dutch psalm must have been heard for blocks around the church building. At last K. S. began to speak. But would anyone be able to understand a man with that voice? First it seemed strange, but after just a few minutes, no one noticed the peculiar voice.

It was obvious that he wrestled with his God during the pastoral prayer. Many wondered, after the editorial in their church paper, whether this man was coming into a lion's den. But he wrestled for the truth! Then he announced as his text Exodus 4:24: "And it came to pass by the way in the inn, that the Lord met him [Moses], and sought to kill him" (KJV). Few people in that immense audience had ever heard a sermon on this curious text. He developed beautifully and deeply all the covenant lines that led to the unusual event and that followed from it. The covenant of grace was clearly presented as God's relationship to humanity and also to Moses. He had no sermon notes with him in the pulpit (he did have the numbers of the psalms to be sung written on a scrap of paper kept in his vest pocket), but he preached for a full hour! It is no hyperbole to say that a person could indeed hear a pin drop during that whole hour. Walking out of the building after the service of that unforgettable Sunday, members of the audience commented about never having heard a sermon like that before. The people of God had been fed and they went home satisfied.

Mention has been made of Schilder's voice, but no other features of his appearance have been noted. Both his preaching and lecturing showed that he became involved with his subject body and soul. The audience had never seen a preacher perspire the way K. S. did, nor had they seen anyone drink as much water during his sermon as he did. After he had preached a few times in an area, the custodians would realize that they had to bring not only a glass of water to the pulpit but a glass plus a pitcher of water. He drank all of it. He was a well-built man who gave the appearance of strength.

K. S. preached several more times during his stay in Grand Rapids. His schedule was about as full as anyone would be able to handle. Typically, he made no effort to avoid any subject. So, he lectured in Rev. Hoeksema's Protestant Reformed church on the subject of common grace, although he knew that he differed from both the CRC and from Hoeksema in his interpretation of the doctrine. On this occasion he gave a beautiful lecture on "Christ in Biblical History." Another of his many speeches was entitled "The Lesson of Thyatira." Whoever heard him preach or lecture was amazed at the well worked-out sermon or lecture he produced. Here was indeed the master at work. There were overflowing crowds wherever he spoke. This was the more remarkable because he always spoke in Dutch (he could read English but had difficulty speaking it). The storm of controversy raised by the notorious editorial in *The Banner* soon subsided. Some churches that had invited him did cancel their invitations after the article appeared, but later there were many more requests for his presence than the host committee could accept. Even the Grand Rapids *Press*, the daily newspaper, carried several articles about the brilliant theologian from Holland and the crowds he was drawing everywhere. Here, too, it can be said that he took the city and area by storm.

K. S. also tried his best, by means of a short conference, to bring together the ministers of the CRC and of the Protestant Reformed Churches (the churches that had followed Rev. H. Hoeksema since 1924). K. S. felt that these two churches ought not to exist separately because both accepted the same confessions. Here ecumenicity must begin. A meeting was held at which ministers of both denominations were in attendance. Hoeksema spoke and set forth his position on the doctrine in question and was ready to speak with the CRC to iron out differences. Then K. S. spoke and emphasized the need for unity. But the conference failed to produce agreement because the Christian Reformed ministers did not appear to be interested in settling differences. Schilder was disappointed. He had hoped that he could be of some service to the churches in the United States by bringing together what belonged together.

K. S. spoke not only in Grand Rapids but was also invited to various other places in western Michigan. He would usually meet first with the Ministers' Conference of the city, speak in one of the churches in the evening, and then preach on Sunday. The reports from all places were again highly laudatory.

Although many more people wanted to hear him or wished to hear him for a second or third time, his schedule demanded that he leave the western Michigan area of the CRC and go west to the other places where the committee had made arrangements for him to speak. First he went to Chicago and from there to Pella, Iowa. He then proceeded to Denver and the west coast. He had a very interesting and busy schedule mapped out for him wherever he went. Of course, he traveled by train. This gave him the time to enjoy the scenery as he sped through the country and to write a journal or diary for *De Reformatie* regarding his American experience. It is interesting to read the comments he made about the country that had opened its arms to him. Through his diary in *De Reformatie*, he kept Dutch church members informed about what he was doing during his months abroad. Reading his regular reports gave an insight into Schilder's almost childlike pleasure in seeing the country he had always hoped to visit and in meeting the Reformed people in it.

Wherever he went in the United States, the result was the same. He was greeted enthusiastically by huge crowds. Ministers in all the different places that he visited commented on the solid Reformed theology articulated by him. Evidently, no one even thought about the notorious editorial in *The Banner* a few months earlier. Moreover, many wondered how there could be opposition to what K. S. taught in his own country and in his own church. Of all the scholars who had come from Holland to the Untied States over the years, perhaps no one made the impression K. S. did. Members of the Christian Reformed Church, the Protestant Reformed Church, and the Reformed Church in America sang the praises of the learned theologian.

After he left the west coast, he retraced his steps and stopped at several places again, including Grand Rapids. The reception in the CRC capital was the same as it had been some months earlier. Enormous crowds came to hear him. His trip to America had indeed been a triumph. But the time had come to return to his home and to his work there. In April of 1939, he made the return voyage to Holland after a visit lasting more than four months.

Professor Greijdanus had taken the place of K. S. as editor-in-chief of *De Reformatie* temporarily while he was in the United States. When Schilder returned he was anxious to take the full load of his paper on his own shoulders again, as well as his work at the theological school. Writers for other religious papers in the country did not welcome him back. They would again have to endure his cutting barbs. Besides, the earlier attempt by editors like H. H. Kuyper to poison the atmosphere in the American Reformed churches had failed miserably. In fact, it had whetted the appetite of the Reformed believers in the United States even more. The tactic had backfired. Schilder had enjoyed himself immensely on his trip, but he was also happy to get back to his family, his work, and the church he loved.

The Synod of Sneek, 1939

As we indicated above, the synod of the GKN meets every three years. It usually meets for a short time and then adjourns provisionally to allow the delegates to work in committees on the tasks assigned to them. Then the entire assembly reconvenes. This manner of conducting synodical business is feasible in the Netherlands because the country is small, and it is not too difficult for the delegates to travel to meetings of the synod several times. While the two previous synods (1933 and 1936) had met under conditions of the worldwide depression, the synod of 1939 met with the danger of war lurking on all sides. Germany had invaded Poland and conquered it quickly. The "phony war," as some had called the earlier situation, had come to an end. It had become obvious that Europe was standing on the brink of general war. Holland was mobilizing its armed forces. When the synod began its sessions, it was already difficult to travel because the trains were being used to transport soldiers and war material. Many proposed that under such conditions the synod should be postponed. It seemed clear that with the threat of war important issues such as the subject matter given the "blue ribbon" committee of 1936 could not be handled in the proper deliberative fashion.

Although postponement seemed the wiser course to a significant number of commentators, they did not fully realize what was going on in the minds of several denominational leaders. One problem was that the report of this famous, or notorious, committee was not written by the committee as a whole. There was no unanimity because, as noted above, at least three members had not met with the others for some time. The synod could face the procedural difficulty of receiving more than one report from the membership of the committee. That is, there could be a majority and more than one minority report. It seemed unlikely that reception of multiple reports would help the synod in easing ecclesiastical tensions that were greater (as H. H. Kuyper had claimed) than in the days before the synod of Assen in 1926. While legitimate questions of these kinds lent support to the movement to postpone the meeting of the synod, several leaders (including some professors from the Free University) had become obsessed with Schilder and considered the 1939 synod to be an opportunity to put him in his place. By raising the issue of nasty journalistic disputes, they had expended much effort to stifle the man they feared and, in some cases, even hated. They were not about to give up now and were, therefore, opposed to the suggestion of postponing the meeting.

The 1939 synod met under trying conditions. There was, of course, pressure from without caused by the military situation and pressure from within because of the deep division in the church. As had been expected, the committee did present majority and minority reports to the synod, but, strangely enough, nothing was heard of the reports either at the synod or later because other matters, which the committee had not studied, were introduced, and they finally determined the actions taken by the synod.

Most of the periodicals in the country urged the synod not to take up the issues contained in the report(s) of the blue ribbon committee. They advocated postponement in the fond hope that the causes for disagreement could be discussed more calmly in less dangerous times. K. S. added his voice to the many others calling for delay, not because he was afraid to face the issues at stake but because he wanted the whole church, i.e., all its members, to be involved in the issues assigned to the blue ribbon committee by the synod of 1936. Needless to say, there were many other more pressing matters that clamored for the synod's attention, such as the dangers to the delegates themselves and to their families if war should come to their land. In the view of K. S., the whole church had to be actively involved in and fully informed about the discussion of any doctrinal differences. They were not for theologians alone to decide, since they would affect the whole church.

The decade of the 1930s, especially the end of it, was a turbulent one indeed, but the churches carried on as well as they could. Individuals on opposite sides of the same issue had done their utmost to cause their views to prevail, but no one had won to this point. This decade had also revealed more clearly than ever before that there were factions and parties in the GKN. The fact that differences existed was to be expected in any denomination.

However, while debates could sharpen the views of members regarding the issues before the denomination, they also had the potential to divide the church. In 1939 it would have taken an almost herculean effort and much good will on both sides to clarify positions without splitting the church.

Chapter 4

The Decade of the Forties

The events of the 1930s had done very little to prepare either the nation or the church for what would happen to them in the 1940s. The synod of 1939, seemingly oblivious to the perils on her path, continued to aggravate the wounds of previous years and make them far more painful than they were before.

The synod turned a deaf ear to the pleas that came from various sources to postpone action on the differences that had surfaced. Although both Schilder and Greijdanus, by reason of their positions as professors of theology (both at Kampen), were advisors of the synod, the majority of the other advisors (most from the Free University) were against them. The synod chose not to wait. The one side, represented by K. S. among others, wanted to discuss differences before a tribunal of the entire church; however, the officers of the synod and the majority of the advisors and delegates were willing to meet in executive session if necessary to accomplish what had been begun in 1936. As it turned out, the synod of 1939 was not able to complete what it had set out to do, but it laid the foundation for further difficulties in the sense that the synod concluded it could do nothing with those questions that the committee appointed in 1936 was to study. Consequently, it moved in a different direction and decided to let a future synod complete the task begun in 1936.

What happened was that the covenant of grace, which had been discussed for many years in the past (long before the present leaders had been born), but which had by no means been at issue for several decades, was placed on the synodical agenda in 1939. That is, in what was supposed to be an effort at bringing the factions together by finding common ground on which all sides could agree, the synod reverted to the Conclusions of Utrecht, adopted by the synod of 1905 when a compromise had been reached on several points of doctrine, including the covenant of grace, and raised this compromise to confessional status. In other words, the synod assigned to it an authority equal to that held by the three confessions that governed the church and its beliefs.

The synod then asked K. S. to sign the compromise document from 1905. This he refused to do because he felt that his signature on the form of subscription—the document that every minister signs indicating his acceptance of the three confessions—was sufficient. Schilder had no objections to the Conclusions of Utrecht as a compromise aimed at satisfying competing parties in 1905, but he refused to sign the document in 1939 because of what he believed his signature on the form of subscription entailed.

When Schilder had achieved a certain prominence as a young minister, he was often troubled by the attitude of some ecclesiastical leaders whom he had always respected. Later, when he had finished his own academic work and had been assigned an important place in the life of the church, he often debated with other leaders who soon discovered that he was more than equal to them. Yet he was especially disturbed by the attitude of the most influential participants in the synodical deliberations of 1939. He did not understand why they ignored the strong sentiment being voiced throughout the country against the handling of potentially divisive issues. As a matter of fact, he was somewhat naive about what was happening all around him. His friends realized much earlier than he that some prominent representatives to the synod wanted to rid the denomination of K. S. He was unable to believe this until the evidence became overwhelming just a few years later.

Each side in the debate of the previous years had a following in the churches. Kuyper and Hepp had many admirers among the disciples of Dr. Abraham Kuyper, even though the two Amsterdam theologians had given some interpretations that were quite at variance with the teachings of the elder Kuyper. K. S. also had a large following. In the mid-1930s, a few ministers in the GKN founded a paper for the purpose of popularizing the teachings of Schilder and the philosophers Dooyeweerd and Vollenhoven; for the new publication, they chose the name *Pro Ecclesia* (= for the church). The very fact that there were these parties in the church did not augur well; the synod, fully aware of the situation, should have done its utmost to heal the breach rather than widen it.

The War Comes to Holland

As has been noted earlier, Holland remained neutral during World War I even though its sympathies seemed to be with Germany more than with the Allies. Her sympathies were also in evidence when Kaiser Wilhelm was given safe haven in the Netherlands after the war in the city of Doorn, where he lived out the remainder of his years in great opulence.

The end of the war had produced an armistice that virtually assured future troubles with Germany. The exceedingly harsh terms imposed on Germany were understandable to some extent because France, which had suffered so terribly during World War I and had also borne the brunt of German aggression in the previous century during the Franco-Prussian War, demanded that the militaristic capabilities of Germany be cut drastically, if not eliminated. The Germans chafed under the difficult terms of the Treaty of Versailles. They had not only been defeated during World War I, but the country also had to endure restrictions that would not have been easy for anyone to tolerate, much less a progressive people like the Germans. One government after another failed to improve the situation. The economy was in a shambles, and the currency of Germany became almost worthless. The situation was ripe for the rise of someone who through whatever means would remove the hated limitations placed on them by the other nations of Europe and the United States of America. Adolf Hitler was the man who stepped into this breach.

Schilder had experienced firsthand the ascendancy of Hitler when he studied at Erlangen from 1930 to 1933. He had examined the ideological background of the Nazi movement and knew that the philosophies of Hegel and Nietzsche were motivating the National Socialists. As he understood the foundations of Naziism, he was not surprised at the excesses to which they led. K. S. had warned the Dutch churches from that time on both in his writings and in speaking. He had strongly backed the decision of the synod of 1936 to discipline members of the GKN who were also members of the National Socialist Party of Holland. The synod had agreed that membership in the church of Christ is incompatible with membership in such a political party. *De Reformatie* had made it plain in many editorials that the political views of Hitler and his party were godless and frightening. The rest of the religious press also condemned Naziism, although perhaps not as strongly as K. S. did in his paper. K. S. mentioned to someone while he was in the United States in 1939 that he knew he was on Hitler's blacklist and that *De Reformatie* had been denied acceptance into Germany for some time.

On May 10, 1940, the blow fell on Holland when Germany invaded the country at several points. A new concept of war was introduced. Disregarding the traditional niceties of declaring war, the Germans ignored their peace treaty with Holland and attacked a peaceful neighbor. The lines of defense that had been set up in European countries proved to be worthless. France had its heralded *Maginot* line and even Holland had its *Greppe Linie*, but when war broke out, the German armies simply went around the French and Dutch defenses and attacked them from the rear. Methods of warfare had changed.

In five days Holland was conquered. Its armed forces had fought valiantly, but the odds were overwhelmingly against them. The army had to lay down its arms, and their small air force had been destroyed. Although there was no opposing air power and there were no antiaircraft guns, the Germans continued to rain bombs on the cities of Holland for five days. The whole center of the city of Rotterdam was destroyed. Thousands of people lost their lives. The royal family was able to escape to England before the German forces took over completely. By May 15 the war was over and Germany ruled the Netherlands.

Holland now had to learn to live under a foreign occupation that would become more harsh as time went on. As part of the reordering of the government, a minister of the GKN was appointed to oversee the religious and church news in the country. This was Dr. H. Vande Vaart Smit, whom Schilder had unmasked long before as a Nazi sympathizer. He was now in the employ of the occupying forces and would both determine what news would go out and scrutinize whatever was published. The whole religious press was now beholden to him. It had not been too daring to condemn the Nazis while they were in Germany and Holland was still a free country. But when the Germans had conquered the country and the Nazis were in control of all government, business, commerce, and the day-to-day life of the people, it became a different matter. The secular press ceased its criticism of the Nazis, and the religious press became very subdued.

Dr. H. H. Kuyper, the editor of *De Heraut*, did not, of course, welcome the Germans into Holland, but he showed a friendly attitude toward them. He had not been in favor of the decision of the synod of 1936 to discipline GKN members who belonged to the Dutch Nazi party and had advised consistories, when they asked him, not to carry out the decision of the synod. He was the professor of church polity at the Free University and had great influence in the churches. It is a remarkable fact that his own son died on the eastern front in Russia fighting on the side of the German forces. Kuyper forfeited his honorable position in the church during the war and was "restored to honor posthumously" after the war. He certainly gave no leadership to the churches in the time of crisis. He also criticized the royal family for escaping Holland to go to England and considered their abandonment of the country neither proper nor heroic. By the end of the war, *De Heraut* as well as *Credo* had ceased to exist. With the secular press no longer free and the religious press nearly mute, there was little opportunity to inform and lead the public in an independent way.

De Reformatie had a different history during World War II. Schilder had written more than anyone else about the evils of National Socialism before the Germans arrived in Holland, and he continued to do so after they had conquered the land. He could not be two-faced. His longstanding motto, taken from the Scriptures, was followed now too: Let your yea be yea and your nay be nay. In sharply worded editorials, he warned the German authorities not to misuse their power because the subjugated people, too, had rights. He warned his own readers not to give up hope but to let the faith they had professed lead them and comfort them now. He wrote several editorials under captions taken from phrases of the Dutch national anthem (*Wilhelmus*) in which he gave some much needed leadership to a public that did not know what to think or do.

People devoured the contents of his paper as soon as it was published. It became so popular that it was sold in the kiosks (book stalls) at railway stations. Never had a religious paper enjoyed such fame and popularity. It was really the only paper in the country that was not only giving positive leadership but was also stirring patriotic feelings by exploiting phrases from the national anthem in a way that both believer and unbeliever were able to understand. He had given leadership to the Reformed in the past on doctrinal and ecclesiastical questions; now he gave the same thorough, thought-provoking guidance to the entire nation on political questions. In this way he endeared himself to many who had not followed him before. His outlook on different questions and his sense of responsibility did not change with the outward changes of the time. The truth did not change and K. S. continued to publish it.

But the German authorities and Vande Vaart Smit also read what Schilder wrote and were furious that anyone had the audacity to write as he did. They obviously could not allow such independence to continue very long. In August 1940, K. S. had written a clearly Reformed editorial in which, using phrases from Dutch poetry, he called on the Lord to come from various directions with his pruning knife to prepare his people for trying times and to deliver them. The German authorities interpreted his words as welcoming the Allies to invade Holland and drive out the Germans.

As a result, they decided it was time to silence K. S. Both the Publishing House of Oosterbaan and Le Cointre and Schilder's own home were raided at the same time. The authorities did extensive damage to the Publishing House, and they destroyed the whole list of subscribers to the paper. Schilder was arrested at his home and taken to a prison cell in the city of Arnhem. K. S. had now begun to suffer directly for his stance against the German forces. It certainly appeared to a large number of observers that he had indeed kept the faith and was now suffering for his fidelity to the truth of God. Kuyper, however, wrote that his imprisonment was not the result of heroic deeds but rather of carelessness. Virtually no one agreed with Kuyper's assessment of the situation. The occupying authorities did allow the totally neutral articles of Kuyper's paper to continue for some time, but the clear voice of *De Reformatie* had been silenced.

Although K. S. did not suffer to the same extent that some of his friends did later in Nazi concentration camps, his pain was very real. For four months he was kept in a prison cell separated from his family, from his work, and from the people whom he loved and who followed him gladly. His work had come to a sudden stop. His religious journalism as well as his teaching and his contributions to the explanation of the Heidelberg Catechism had to be halted.

Here sat a man who was accustomed to working day and night and who now had only his thoughts for his companions. He knew that he was suffering for his faith. The Germans had feared his pen more than foreign soldiers. People throughout the country were in daily prayer for the release of this humble child of God who was also their champion in the faith.

His release came without advance announcement in December 1940. The synods of the GKN had always appointed committees to deal with church matters that would affect the government, and Dr. H. H. Kuyper was the chairman of this committee. Schilder, in his naïveté, believed that Kuyper had been responsible for his release and promptly sent him a thank-you letter. He received no response to his letter, and he really did not think that one was required. However, sometime later one of the ministers of the GKN showed Schilder a letter that Kuyper had written to him. From the letter it became painfully clear that Kuyper, by not working for his release, was responsible, not for K. S.'s freedom, but rather for the length of time he was imprisoned. Kuyper's unfortunate way of dealing with another minister of the same denomination also affected a large number of people who looked to *De Reformatie* for guidance. His actions likewise raise questions about how he dealt with the honor of his own country. There may have been differences of opinion and insight, but it must be admitted that this was an extraordinary way for a clergyman to treat a colleague.

When the German authorities released Schilder, they forbade him to write anything. Their threat was that should he pen something for public consumption, he would be arrested and placed in a concentration camp in Germany. They were determined to prevent K. S. from writing the kind of editorials he had published in the summer of 1940. They refused to allow him to encourage a large group of people to oppose the teachings and authority of the Third Reich.

In the months and years that followed, Schilder's experience was varied. There were occasions when he would go to Kampen for a few days to teach his students; at another time for unknown reasons, the Germans had issued an order to shoot him on sight. Most of the time between December 1940 and the early part of 1944, he had to be in hiding and regularly on the move throughout the country to save his life. He would live on farms of people who were his supporters in the northern provinces, but as soon as anyone would recognize him, he had to find another safe house. Once when he was staying at a particular farm for a few weeks, a neighbor said to the lady of the house, "It is remarkable how much your boarder looks like Prof. Schilder." With his hiding place discovered, it was definitely time to move again. Toward the end of his vagabond years, he spent some time in the home of his good friend, Dr. P. Jasperse, in the city of Leiden. Here his friends brought him some books so that at least he had something profitable to do. Throughout the war years, his partisans brought food to the place where he stayed so that he could maintain his health.

Throughout this entire period, the synod (of 1939) kept meeting. The Nazi government had silenced Schilder; he also faced opposition within his denomination in which he continued to be influential. Strange to say, the synod of 1939, meeting during the war years, attached the greatest importance to finding a method by which K. S. could be muzzled. As we have seen, the doctrinal differences identified by the synod of 1936 and the following committee reports did not satisfy the delegates to the 1939 synod. A new procedure was suggested and finally adopted in order to break the impasse. The synod decided to change the status of the Conclusions of Utrecht, a document formulated as compromise in 1905 and advocating among other points presumed regeneration (that is, the children of believers are presumed to be born again until the opposite appears). It elevated the document to the status of a confession; as a result, all office bearers were required to signify their agreement with the Conclusions of Utrecht as well as with the confessions.

While it is true that all office bearers in the church were affected by the synodical decision, there is little doubt that it was aimed primarily at Schilder because his opponents knew that he would not be able to sign the Conclusions. He not only believed that it was wrong to elevate the Conclusions to confessional status, but he also had grave difficulties with their contents. Two synodical delegates who did not agree with the decision to make a new demand of office bearers and hence of Schilder, were asked to leave the meetings of the assembly. Needless to say, expelling the opposition was an unusual way to achieve unity, and the legality of dismissing properly elected delegates was also suspect. Both Schilder and Prof. S. Greijdanus wrote letters to the synod urging the delegates not to change the status of the Conclusions because doing so would have serious consequences for the church and could divide it. But the synod was deaf to all such appeals.

Finally, toward the end of 1942, Schilder wrote a letter to his own consistory in Kampen and then to all the consistories of the denomination, arguing that the current synod was no longer a legal one. The synod of 1939, under normal procedure, should by this time have given way to the synod of 1942. He concluded that the actions of the present synod were not to be considered authoritative because of church order Article 31, which stipulates that decisions of ecclesiastical assemblies are settled and binding unless it is demonstrated that they conflict with the word of God or the church order. Since the synod of 1939 had exceeded the prescribed three-year time limit, it did not conform with the church order and its decisions therefore were not official.

It must be remembered that the delegates to the synod were working under difficult conditions. Travel to and from the meetings of the synod could be dangerous and was complicated by the fact that the railway system in Holland, one of the best in the world, was no longer dependable. The president of the synod of 1939, Rev. J. Schouten, had died soon after the meetings began. The representatives were torn in two directions. The leaders and the great majority of delegates wished to find a solution to the "Schilder problem," but there were others who feared what would happen to the churches if he were attacked. On one occasion Schilder was even able to receive a small committee of the synod in the home in which he was staying. He urged the delegates not to continue in the direction the synod had begun to go. But it was all in vain.

The 1939 synod kept meeting well into the time when the synod of 1942 should have been constituted, and it approved the plan to give the Conclusions of Utrecht confessional standing. It took some time before the details were finalized. In fact a synod of 1942 was elected, and it continued the "progress" made by the previous synod. Not until the spring of 1944 were the decisions of the synod made known to the public as a result of the action of the 1942 Synod. All the work of the two synods was necessarily done without the knowledge of the members of the GKN because, due to censorship of the religious press, no one could reach them with the written word. Controversies could not be explained nor could the different points of view be defended or refuted in the press. Unavoidable secrecy was a regrettable feature of the manner in which the synod had conducted its business.

On March 23 K. S., who had refused to signify his assent to the Conclusions of Utrecht, received the official report of the synod that he had been suspended from his position as professor of theology at Kampen and as emeritus minister of the church at Rotterdam Delfshaven. His own consistory at Kampen, where his membership resided, had not been consulted nor had the consistory of Delfshaven, which held his ministerial credentials. The fact that this decision was made "from above" and without consulting local ecclesiastical bodies was an example of the new church polity supported a few years earlier by Dr. H. H. Kuyper when he approved the doctoral thesis of M. Bouwman. Schilder again was hurt and dumbfounded. He had never thought that the synod would go so far. His first words were, "So, they have dared to do this." Then he sat down at the parlor organ in the home of Dr. Jasperse and played and sang Psalm 51, David's song of penitence and lament. He was deeply wounded. The denomination, for which he had given his whole life and which had also honored him with one of its highest positions, had now suspended him. And for what reason? For defending what he understood to be the truth of the Scriptures and the faith of the fathers. He wondered whether such a stance was to be considered criminal in the church from now on.

Schilder knew from the outset that he could not sign the Conclusions of Utrecht, or any part of them, as though they were equal to the confessions. This was a church polity question. But he also had theological questions concerning the Conclusions. He did not believe that they accurately presented the views of Scripture on several points such as the doctrine of the covenant. For him, all who are baptized are included in the covenant—a point not expressed in the Conclusions of Utrecht. They taught that baptized individuals who later demonstrated that they were unbelievers were not actually in the covenant as a communion of life. Questions of doctrine and church polity are very close together, the one being scarcely distinguishable from the other at times, and both definitely came into play in this controversy. K. S. would write exhaustively on the matter in subsequent years.

Suspension does not mean dismissal, and the period of its duration is intended to inspire reflection and repentance. K. S. did indeed reflect, but he did not repent. He had no intention of giving up his life's work for what he considered some poorly formulated doctrinal propositions of a synod and for church polity views that had never been accepted by the church. As soon as he was able to write again in late 1945, he carefully unraveled the whole synodical formulation for the benefit of church members. Those who had drawn up this formulation were shown to be mere infants in matters of dogmatics, when the master began to dissect the report. It is significant that nothing is reported about the contribution of Dr. V. Hepp in connection with the work of the synod. Hepp died in 1950, never having regained the important place he once held in the hearts and minds of the people of the GKN. Hepp's once promising life turned out to be one of some frustration.

As has been noted, Schilder had been suspended from office on March 23, 1944. There seemed little hope that the synod would retract its decision regarding K. S. because too many delegates at the synod, and especially its leadership wanted to be rid of this gadfly once and for all. There were peculiar rumors floating around that interpreted his actions during the war in a highly unfavorable light. He had often been invited to appear at the meetings of the synods of 1939 and 1942, but he had always declined, saying that the authorities would not permit him to appear in public. He was accused of fabricating the story that he was unable to be present at the synod because of the German edict. It seems that the accusations arose because he did in fact surface at times and did publish some articles during the years in question.

His opponents repeated the charge against him, although there was some contrary documentation. He had written to the board of the Kampen theological school about his situation in 1940 after he had been released from the prison at Arnhem. The board had urged him to go underground and not risk his life. At least two of the board members were delegates to the synod of 1939 and obviously well aware of the board's recommendations. It is difficult to see the logic followed by the delegates who should have known better; moreover, little brotherly love seems to have been displayed by the delegates who wanted to rid themselves of so prominent a churchman. After all, K. S. had worked diligently for the welfare of the churches for many years and had done more to build up the faith of the Reformed people than almost anyone else.

There is just so much time an ecclesiastical body is able to give to a suspended office bearer. Three months after his suspension, the synod, seeing no signs of repentance, decided to depose

Dr. Prof. Klaas Schilder as a minister of the gospel and as a professor of theology. In addition, the emeritated Dr. Professor S. Greijdanus, who had written letters to the synod defending Prof. Schilder, was also deposed. The synod thus deposed two of the denomination's most gifted and most loyal servants. The reasons given for their dismissal lacked substance. The statements these two professors were asked to sign were withdrawn by the synod less than two years later. This sequence of events suggests that the statements were not so important in themselves; rather, they served as an efficient means for getting rid of K. S. whom the delegates thought of as a troublemaker, a tenacious opponent who refused to drop or tone down an argument until everyone was exhausted.

Could the Church Go On?

Between the time of his suspension and his deposition, K. S. often wondered how he would be able to make a living after his deposition became final. The question was hardly an idle one. When he was deposed, he was fifty-three years old and still had many family responsibilities. What was a deposed, middle-aged minister and professor able to do to earn a living? He concluded that he would become a freelance writer after the war ended. Yet he realized that, though his writings had been popular in the past, his publications as a deposed minister and professor might not be received very readily by church members. At best, he anticipated, it would be a meager living. He had been deeply wounded. He knew the church would suffer from the effects of the synod, and now even his own livelihood was actually in question. He was torn as few Reformed scholars have ever been.

The synod had dealt with him as a rebel, as a person who had stirred up mutiny in the church, as an individual who was "a disgrace to the church," a "rotten member" (his own words). All the flowery words said about him in later years could not erase from his heart and mind what the synod had said about him officially. He reminded the president of the synod, Dr. G. Berkouwer, that, regardless how many impressive books Berkouwer wrote, it did not change the fact that his name was signed to the deposition papers handed to K. S. in 1944.

The deposition of Schilder proved to be only the first in a series of depositions. The synod dispatched a letter that was to be read in all the churches of the denomination, informing the members that K. S. was no longer a minister or professor in the GKN. Some took this to be good news; others were disturbed by it. K. S., of course, had a following. His journalistic labors of many years soon produced fruit. Thousands of readers, both clergy and lay, had been instructed by the writings of Schilder in the past, and they found it incredible that he had suddenly become a heretic. When the grounds for the deposition became known, Schilder's partisans were more troubled. A sizable number of ministers and elders, therefore, refused to sign their assent to the covenantal teachings in the Conclusions of Utrecht as being equal to the confessions. The synod had apparently not anticipated that others besides K. S. and the elderly Greijdanus would object to its decision and thus become candidates for synodical discipline. Now, however, the problem was spreading.

Consequently, the decision of the synod had to be applied to many other ordained church officers. They, too, had to be deposed or the synod would appear arbitrary, thus bringing into question why it had deposed Schilder. The novel church polity adopted by Dr. H. H. Kuyper in 1938 had been used by the synods of 1939 and 1942. According to Reformed church order before 1938, only consistories were allowed to exercise discipline. Should it become necessary to discipline an officer, the consistory of his church together with a neighboring consistory was to judge the matter. In 1944 the various classes and the synod took over the responsibility for disciplining church officers.

It had also been a rule of Reformed church polity that a disciplining body could exercise its authority on only one individual at a time. Even if a husband and wife became subject to discipline, they were to be judged individually and not as a couple. In 1944 the denomination proceeded differently. In the large city of Groningen, the synod disciplined three ministers and more than fifty elders in one action. In the city of Amersfoort, something similar happened: two ministers and more than fifty elders were subjected to discipline through a single decision. These were not the only examples. As the saying went, it rained depositions in Holland for months.

In a comparatively short time, two hundred churches broke away from the GKN. A significant number of the most able ministers left or were deposed. The 1942 Synod had obviously not expected such a massive reaction, and it now seemed to be helpless after the move against Schilder produced large-scale repercussions. It seemed as though nothing would be able to stanch the bleeding. In time a total of 10 percent, or 100,000 members, left the GKN because of the actions of the 1942 synod. In other words, the exodus from the denomination became larger than the secession of 1834 or the *Doleantie* of 1886.

It is difficult to understand why an able historian such as Dr. L. Praamsma says in his book *Het Dwaze Gods* (p. 377) that K. S. should have appeared at the sessions of the synod and defended himself as professor of dogmatics and as leader of a large segment of the church if he really wished to preserve truth and unity. "Professor Schilder chose a different route," he says (translation mine). However, Praamsma overlooks the fact that Schilder had to remain underground, a statement that can be documented. Since he could not meet safely with the synod, it is unfair to say he chose a different route; it was the synod that chose the way.

Now that thousands of members had elected to break ranks with the GKN, a new situation had developed. What was to become of all these former GKN members? A decision was made to hold a meeting at The Hague on August 11, 1944; all who had been deposed or had left the GKN voluntarily were invited to attend. There was an enormous response. No Reformed church was large enough to hold all the people who came, so the meeting was held in the large Lutheran church. The meeting was under the chairmanship of the Rev. H. Knoop, a longtime friend and colleague of Schilder who had spent a lengthy period during the war in the concentration camp at Dachau and had suffered almost beyond human endurance.

K. S. read a statement, which he himself had formulated, advocating withdrawal and return, that is, withdrawal from their former denomination (the GKN) and a return to the confessions and the church order of Dort. His statement was accepted enthusiastically. The gathering also decided to establish a new theological school in Kampen as the existing Kampen theological school now stood in opposition to the seceders. With this decision all Schilder's fears about how he would earn a living were put to rest. He, together with Prof. Greijdanus and Dr. R. J. Dam, formerly a lecturer at Kampen, were invited to become the faculty of the new school. Schilder was ready, of course, to accept this new challenge. Greijdanus, though already retired, was willing to come out of retirement to resume his teaching of New Testament subjects. But it was 1944 and the Germans still occupied Holland. Dr. Dam was murdered by the Germans shortly before the liberation and consequently never had a chance to teach at the new theological school.

Disorganization and Organization

While the Germans continued to occupy the country, the populace suffered greatly in 1944–45, the last winter of the war. It was a harsh winter. Food and fuel were in dangerously short supply, and many people there had no choice but to trade heirlooms for a crust of bread. But if conditions were difficult in the social and economic life, they certainly were no better in the ecclesiastical arena. The churches, which had for such a long time enjoyed great spiritual prosperity, now found themselves bleeding and even hemorrhaging. In some places almost the entire congregation left the GKN and joined what were soon called "the liberated churches." In other places, a few office bearers and only some of the congregation left. In still others, just a handful of people joined the new federation. Disunity in the churches soon led to divisions within families and between friends.

The "liberated" quickly began to found Christian schools of their own. The Anti-Revolutionary Party, the political party that Dr. A. Kuyper had founded, was split, and another that favored the teaching of the liberated churches was formed. Seldom, if ever, has the Reformed community in Holland seen such disruption. Principles have their effects and demand consequences. No leader of the GKN had ever dreamt that the decisions of the 1939 and 1942 Synods would cause so much difficulty. They had failed to read accurately the minds and feelings of their own members and had underestimated the number of Prof. Schilder's admirers. The GKN recovered numerically from the secession of 1944, but it would never recover the spiritual depth it had lost as a result of the synodical decisions.

Once the decision was made that there would be a new denomination, attention had to be given to questions of organization. It is not easy to set up an organization as complex as a denomination. It is true that there were entire consistories that had left the GKN, and the members of these consistories were usually immediately installed in the new "liberated" churches. In other places officers had to be elected in churches where no elders or deacons had left their former denomination. However, while there were consistories, there were at first no *classes* or synod. The complete bureaucracy of the GKN had also ceased to exist for those who now began anew.

The kinds of questions that usually accompany denominational splits surfaced almost at once. Who has a right to the money and property of the churches to which the "liberated" had formerly belonged? Did they belong to the members who elected to remain in the GKN, or, if a majority of members opted to leave, did they control the congregation's resources? Such financial disagreements often had to be settled in the secular courts. In some instances the courts made rulings only to reverse them later. Some of the "liberated" were forced to meet in makeshift buildings for their worship services. Although many ministers had joined the new denomination, there were far more places where preaching services were required than there were ministers to fill them. Some pastors preached four and more times per Sunday before different audiences. The "liberated" churches grew dramatically. Naturally there were areas of the country where the new denomination grew much faster than in others, but it would be misleading to say that it was only a local or regional movement.

Schilder was very happy in the new church. Here he felt he could breathe again. He was also surprised and ecstatic that so many of the laity and clergy had freed themselves from the yoke of the GKN. He was bitterly disappointed with the attitude of some colleagues who seemingly had agreed with him for many years but had decided to stay in the GKN. He could not understand that men such as Dr. S. G. De Graaf, Dr. R. Schipper, and others did not join the "liberated." There had, of course, been other cases in which leaders had been extremely dissatisfied with conditions in a church but had chosen to remain in it. For example, Groen van Prinsterer did not go along with the movement headed by Hendrik De Cock in 1834, even though he was sympathetic to the people of the secession. Nor did all of Abraham Kuyper's friends follow him at the time of the *Doleantie*. Such individuals echoed the sentiments of Erasmus: "I am not made of the stuff of reformers."

It had been made clear at the meeting in The Hague on August 11, 1944 that the "liberated" wanted theological training of students to continue in Kampen. A group of churches, resembling a *classis*, met together later in 1944 and specified more exactly the kind of training the new denomination expected for the men who were preparing for the ministry. A building was purchased in Kampen to serve as a theological school. Extensive remodeling had to be done, but there was no time to lose because the churches needed ministers. Schilder and Greijdanus began to teach as soon as possible. But a theological school with two professors is not much of a school.

A synod was called together in 1945 to take up the matter of appointing men to teach at the new school. The synod did not go outside of its own denominational membership to find men who would be capable of filling "the vacancies created by the unfaithfulness of the professors Ridderbos, Dijk and Den Hartogh." These were K. S.'s own words, written when he was arguing for the necessity of three appointments to the new theological school. None of the three men who were appointed had advanced academic degrees, but all three were extremely capable, seasoned, and thoroughly Reformed.

The Rev. Benne Holwerda of Amersfoort was chosen to teach Old Testament subjects; the Rev. C. Veenhof, who had most recently served a church in Utrecht, was appointed to teach practical theology; and the Rev. P. Deddens of Groningen was selected to teach church history and church polity. Though the faculty was too small, it was of the same size as the one at the GKN's theological school in Kampen. Schilder had pleaded for a sixth professor at the GKN's Kampen school long before the war, but the proposal had always been turned down because of the cost. The three professors chosen by the first "liberated" synod (1945) handled well their assignments of teaching and giving leadership in the denomination. Three lecturers were also chosen by the first "liberated" synod, and it answered affirmatively the age-old question of "Promotie Recht," the right of Kampen to give advanced academic degrees.

Schilder was simply delighted at this turn of events. It was beyond his fondest expectations that a few federation of churches should spring from the old denomination, which he thought was more and more becoming a false church. He was also pleased with the founding of a new theological school in which he and his friend and spiritual father of many years, Dr. S. Greijdanus, would play leading roles. He had always considered Greijdanus to be completely dependable, even at the time when he found few others on whom he could rely. He admired his friend's ability and his genuine piety. He knew the new professors quite well and was thoroughly satisfied that they were the ones designated for the posts. That "Promotie Recht" was also given simply crowned with glory what was for him a most successful synod. He felt that he had received far more than he could have expected.

Belgium was freed by the Allied forces some time before Holland was liberated. The Netherlands was finally freed of the German occupation on May 5, 1945. The damage the Germans had done to the Dutch economy in the first weeks of the war was incalculable. They even tried to move all the rolling stock of the railroads to Germany, but they did not succeed. A large number of Dutch people lost their lives in the last few days when the Germans were present. The murder of Dr. Dam has already been mentioned, but there were many others who paid with their lives when the possibility of German victory was long past. Human life meant little to the barbaric conquerors.

At the end of the war, the country could finally breathe again even though much of it lay in ruins. The whole economy, which had been strong before the war, had to be rebuilt. The social structure in Holland had been severely tested during the war. In the ecclesiastical sphere, perhaps the greatest damage had been done to the structure of the GKN, one of the largest Reformed bodies in

Holland. But the church goes on—if not under a well-known name of the past, then under a new name that holds to the confessions of the past. The GKN, however, would never be the same. It had not only lost many members but had also shifted positions radically (for example, regarding church polity), and these changes would be determinative in the future. The denomination had not just rid itself of someone its leaders considered a troublemaker; it had lost far more. This is not putting it too strongly. The individuals who would not sign their agreement in 1944 to giving the Conclusions of Utrecht the status of the confessions were not allowed to serve as officers in the GKN.

However, a decade or two later, clergy who denied cardinal doctrines of Christianity were allowed in its pulpits, and they were kept in good standing in the church. Inevitably, when an organization undergoes major change, it has significant consequences for some time to come. History serves to warn all those who study it. In this case, candidates who had received their training at the denomination's theological schools were barred from ordination in the church if they refused to assent to the sixteen points that the synod had drawn up to explain the Conclusions of Utrecht. Professors were called on to help classes in examining candidates.

One candidate, H. J. Schilder (a nephew of K. S.), had accepted a call from a congregation. He was denied ordination, and the church that called him was read out of the denomination after it refused to accept the *classis's* decision not to ordain candidate Schilder. Both the synod and the different classes continued to exercise discipline over officers. In the light of these developments, the significance of Greijdanus's vote against the discipline of Geelkerken in 1926 becomes very clear. Though he had agreed that Geelkerken's position was inconsonant with the creeds, Greijdanus realized that a synod had no right to depose him. Only his own consistory could do that. Traditional Reformed principles of church polity were violated in 1926 and certainly in 1944. The drastic changes in the way in which the church disciplined its officers had moved the center of ecclesiastical authority from the local level, where the details and personalities in a case would be known most completely, to regional and national bodies, which were further removed from it.

Postwar Problems

To a large extent, the members of the churches were still in the dark about the reason for the split of 1944 and the consequences it might have in their lives. The religious press was almost nonexistent. There was really no dependable means for instructing the members about the far-reaching decisions of the synod. The denominational leaders still had to be careful in their public speaking during 1944 and the first months of 1945. Evidence of the danger is seen in Dr. Dam's murder only a month before the country was liberated. For obvious reasons, everything had been done secretively. The synod had made its decision when editors were not able to inform readers. Besides, both *De Heraut* and *Credo* had ceased to exist during the war, and *De Reformatie* had been forbidden to publish.

It was not until August 1945, almost exactly five years after it had been banished by the German authorities, that *De Reformatie* appeared again. K. S. was still the editor, but the long list of correspondents (that is, the regular writers), numbering almost a hundred in the summer of 1940, no longer appeared. True, some writers who had not changed their allegiance to Schilder since 1940 once again contributed, but their names were not printed in the masthead. That would come later. The editor had to be very sure anyone listed in the masthead was indeed a supporter of what he had always wanted and was still seeking to accomplish. He had learned that some correspondents whose names appeared in the masthead of the paper in 1940 had voted for his deposition.

The sharpness of the editor's pen had not been blunted during the years when the paper *De Reformatie* was banned. Readers recognized the same emphases with which they had been familiar since 1929. Different subjects, however, now called for K. S.'s attention. He informed the readership about what had happened in the church struggle of 1939 to 1944 by printing the official documents in his paper. As always, he was very forthright in laying the blame where he thought it belonged. He gave his readers an insight into the workings of the blue ribbon committee of 1936. He explained to them some of the secret actions that had been taken in the last few years and that would affect all of them. He made clear how the "liberated" churches had fared since August 1944. He had his paper again, and through this medium he could reach the membership of the church.

As he saw the situation, the leaders of the GKN could continue to do their work, but he for his part would inform the people who were "shepherded" by such leaders. The paper began haltingly because the subscription list had been destroyed by the Germans in August 1940. It was also very difficult to obtain materials for publishing a paper or magazine. But the subscribers who received the paper after a five-year hiatus were happy to have their familiar friend in their homes again.

The New Theological School

During the last days of the war, Schilder had been able to instruct Kampen students, but he had to do his teaching in the city of Groningen. It was hit and miss. There was no continuity in the instruction because of the uncertain and difficult times. However, when the war had ended and the first synod of the liberated churches had dealt especially with questions affecting the theological school, the way was opened to return to the old city of Kampen. The address was no longer *Oudestraat*, but *Broederweg*. Both the school of the synodical churches (GKN) and the school of the "liberated" churches would from now on be found in the same city.

The larger part of the student body from the old Kampen theological school had joined the "liberated" churches and chose to continue their studies under the teaching of K. S. and his colleagues. The school began with an enrollment of thirty-four students. These young men were fully aware of the fact that their professional lives might well be spent ministering to small congregations. But they were convinced their cause was worthy. They, no more than their professors, wished to be under the dominion of a synod that had drastically changed church polity. For Schilder, times seemed to have returned almost to normal. He could write in his own paper again, and he could teach students together with those who shared his views of the Scriptures and confessions. He did not have to be afraid that board members would seek to undermine his influence, as had happened when he taught at the GKN's theological school in Kampen. The early days of the liberation had for him indeed been a liberation. Liberation, however, did not mean a lighter schedule of work. Not only did his teaching load and his journalistic duties cry out for his time, he was also preaching several times virtually every Sunday. When a group needed advice, K. S. was called; when a group needed a speaker, K. S. was called. He had never been busier, but he had also never enjoyed himself as much.

From the first year the new Kampen school was in session, an annual *Schooldag* (= school day) was held for the benefit of the theological school. On a prescribed day in September, members of the "liberated" churches would come by car or by bus from all parts of the country to celebrate with the board, faculty, and student body the opening of another school year. Meetings were held in almost all the larger churches in Kampen, and the professors and some of the more prominent ministers would speak. The numbers of people attending were in the thousands. The *Schooldag* brought the school and the church membership close together.

At the meetings large offerings were taken and were designated for the library fund of the school. A women's auxiliary was formed throughout the country; it, too, worked to supply funds for the library. It is an enormous undertaking to establish a new theological school, and the library is an essential but expensive element of one. Soon the fledgling school could boast of a large selection of books thanks to the diligent efforts and generosity of so many people. The common member of the church thus also learned to know the professors of the school. Through events such as the school day, the theological school of the "liberated" churches attained a position among the constituency of the church, which has seldom been duplicated—a situation that served the welfare of both the school and the churches.

The Mid to Late 1940s

For many years attempts had been made to have an organization of all reformed churches worldwide. Dr. V. Hepp had, as noted earlier, made some attempts in this direction in 1929 and again in the early 1930s. However, his attempts had not succeeded because they were not well thought out, nor did they conform with the positions of the GKN in the sense that the board appointed had included members who supported Geelkerken, the minister who had been condemned as holding unreformed positions about the first chapters of Genesis. The Reformed churches in South Africa had discussed Reformed ecumenicity since 1924. The Christian Reformed Church had sent representatives to the Synod of Sneek of the GKN meeting in 1939, and the Reformed Church of South Africa had also sent fraternal delegates to that synod. Before the synod took up the internal matters that have been described above, it had voted its approval of a Reformed Ecumenical Synod that would meet in Holland. With all the difficulties caused by the outbreak of war, nothing came of its noble plan. However the representatives from North America and South Africa brought the news of the GKN synod's decision to their own respective synods. Both of these synods agreed with the concept.

After the war, in 1946, the first Reformed Ecumenical Synod met in Grand Rapids, Michigan. It was hosted by the Christian Reformed Church because the situation in Holland was not advantageous for having such a body meet there in the early period after the war. However, only two other denominations had been invited to this the Reformed Ecumenical Synod: Die Gereformeerde Kerken in Suid-Africa and the GKN. The Christian Reformed Church invited the *synodical* Gereformeerde Kerken because that was the only similarly conservative Reformed denomination it knew in Holland. Communications still had not been fully reestablished. The denomination in North America really did not know what had happened in the Dutch ecclesiastical world during the war, although there was some awareness that a dispute had taken place. The editor of *The Banner* opined that the difficulty must have centered on the doctrine of common grace, but his hunch showed only how little he knew.

Schilder was not very happy that the synodical church had been invited while the "liberated" had been ignored. He was confident, nevertheless, that at the meeting of the ecumenical synod the misunderstanding would be rectified. K. S. felt that both the Christian Reformed Church and the Church of South Africa should be apprised of the happenings in the Dutch churches during the war. Once they understood what had transpired, a future RES (Reformed Ecumenical Synod) might well invite the "liberated" churches rather than the GKN.

When the ecumenical synod met, it could not escape the question of the history of the Reformed churches in Holland during the war. Article 26 of the *Acts of the First Reformed Ecumenical Synod* reads:

Dr. G. C. Berkouwer elucidates the ecclesiastical difficulties in the Netherlands. Since Professor Berkhof (president of this Synod) cannot be present, the Vice-President, Dr. Aalders, presides. No one desires that Synod meet in closed session. Dr. Berkouwer proceeds with a review of the most important events in the Gereformeerde Kerken during the last ten years. The General Synod of 1936 had appointed a committee to study various controversial questions. To the satisfaction of many, certain conclusions were reached in 1942 by unanimous vote. In the same year, however, *gravamina* against the Conclusions of Utrecht of 1905 were presented to Synod. Synod did not sustain these *gravamina* but declared that the Conclusions were in harmony with Scripture and Confession. It also declared that the Conclusions were binding upon all concerned. This led at last to the deposition of Professor K. Schilder. Synod came to this final step in the interest of good order in the Church of Jesus Christ. The Synod of Utrecht of 1946 gave a new formulation of the Conclusions of 1905. The Christian Reformed Church in America was not consulted, not because Synod did not feel the need of such consultation, but because of the great urgency of the situation.

Members of Synod make use of the opportunity to ask questions pertaining to the situation in the sister Churches in the Netherlands.

The Synod took up this matter a short time later and this is the official version: (Art. 39, RES Acts, 1946):

"Esteemed Fathers and Brethren:

Your Committee has the following to report regarding 'III, Ecclesiastical Difficulties in the Netherlands':

I. Formal Aspects of this Question:

Your Committee, having received a mandate from Synod (Cf. Article 24, "Conclusions, Recommendations 4"), advises Synod to declare that it has the authority to take up the case of Ecclesiastical Difficulties in the Churches of the Netherlands since:

1. Synods may assist member Churches of the Ecumenical Synod in their difficulties when requested to do so; a principle already embodied in the principles the Reformed Churches of the Netherlands and the Christian Reformed Church have laid down in inter-church correspondence.

2. No review of concrete disciplinary cases is required of us, and
3. Synod should be an assembly to which doctrinal appeals may be addressed.
Adopted.

II. Material Aspects of This Question: (Art. 62, Acts RES)

The matter to be discussed is found in 'III, A.B.C.,' p. 5 of our mimeographed report (Article 24).

Concerning 'A Gravamen has been introduced against the decision of the Synod of 1905, Sub 4. Synod has judged the decisions in harmony with Scripture and Confession. Was this right?', your Committee wishes to call to mind the following historical facts:

A. The Christian Reformed Church of America has ratified the Conclusions of Utrecht of 1905 in its decision of 1908.
B. At no time were any Scriptural objections addressed to the Synod against point 4.
C. The South African Churches have never officially adopted the Conclusions of 1905.

Your Committee advises Synod to reply to the Synod of the Reformed Churches of the Netherlands that this Ecumenical Synod cannot give an answer to this question since it lacks the necessary time to take adequate cognizance of the gravamen presented to the Synod of the Netherlands and of the reports occasioned by this gravamen. Moreover, in the judgment of Synod, Synod should limit itself to a formulation of opinion with respect to the "Declarations of the 1946 Synod" without entering into the concrete difficulties of the Reformed Churches of the Netherlands, and therefore should leave the Utrecht Conclusions as much as possible in the background, particularly since these have been superseded by the "Declarations of the 1946 Synod."
Adopted.

Concerning "III, B. Even if it (Synod of the Reformed Churches) might not be right, would this justify a rupture in the Church?", your Committee proposes the following advice: Synod inform the Reformed Churches of the Netherlands that in its judgment, in case one is convinced that a Synod makes an unwarrant-

90

ed doctrinal pronouncement, he is not justified to bring about a rupture, unless he has exhausted all the possibilities provided by the Church Order for procuring a revision and the Church persists in maintaining its position contrary to his conviction concerning the truth.

Adopted.

Concerning "III, C. What is our evaluation of the declaration which the Reformed Churches of the Netherlands formulated re the covenant of grace and baptism?", your Committee advises Synod to appoint a special Committee to investigate and to report to this Synod whether the declarations of 1946 conform with the Scriptures and the Confessions.

Adopted.

It cannot be charged that the Reformed Ecumenical Synod condemned the position of the "liberated" churches in a formal sense. However, the fact that the "liberated" churches were not asked to send representatives to this first ecumenical synod was, as noted above, in part due to ignorance of the situation, and in part due to the fact that no inquiry was made before the RES met. The GKN delegates were asked to provide information for the other churches represented at the meeting regarding the ecclesiastical history of the Reformed churches in Holland during the 1940s. The position of the "liberated" churches and the theological position of Prof. Schilder were in fact condemned at this synod. Schilder had in effect been judged, indicted, and condemned without being heard. Due process would have called for the synod to contact the "liberated" churches or even K. S. himself to obtain additional information about the case.

For the GKN to ask the first Reformed Ecumenical Synod whether it would justify "a rupture" in the church if the GKN synod had not been right in its formulations of doctrinal positions in 1944, is telling. These formulations were used to discipline and depose officers in the church, and candidates for the ministry were threatened if they would not in every way adhere to the teachings found in them. Was there the possibility that these statements might not be correct? At the same time, the GKN made it clear to everyone that Schilder had caused the "rupture," even though the church had deposed him. The RES, by agreeing that no "rupture" was justified even though the formulations had not been right, agreed that the "victim" had caused the "rupture." Here one sees how decisions based on incomplete information can do significant damage to churches.

Schilder was disturbed and hurt by the lack of true church "style" as he now saw it develop. He had expected better from both the Christian Reformed Church and the Reformed Churches of South Africa. He had made many friends in the United States during his trip in 1939. But the sad fact was that he was being isolated more and more. The fact that he had opposed the leaders in the denomination he serviced, had not been treated kindly in his own country, and he now perceived that their influence extended far beyond the borders of Holland. He made a strong appeal to the *Christelijke Gereformeerde Kerk* to join the liberated churches. After all, this small denomination, too, denied the view of presumptive regeneration, which the GKN had raised to confessional status. The *Christelijke Gereformeerde Kerk* did join the RES later, but it did not affiliate with the "liberated" churches.

In 1947 K. S. was again invited to visit the United States. The invitation did not come from a CRC committee as it had in 1938— far from it. This time it came from the Protestant Reformed Church. He accepted the invitation, but before he arrived in the United States, the "Synodical Committee" of the Christian Reformed Church placed an ad in *The Banner*, urging the churches not to invite Schilder to preach in CRC pulpits and not to invite him to speak during the week. The committee's action made it crystal clear how the CRC felt about him and the churches he served. Although there was no formal statement in which the position of Prof. Schilder was condemned, it had become obvious that the CRC considered the "synodical" churches to be the true continuation of the GKN. At best, Schilder was negated. When Schilder heard what the "committee" had done, he asked: "What is that?" Neither he nor the GKN knew of any "committee" that functioned as the CRC synodical committee did. It was a group that apparently spoke for the whole denomination while the synod was not in session.

K. S. was warmly welcomed by the Protestant Reformed Churches. He had met the Rev. H. Hoeksema in 1939 and had had long conversations with him at that time. They had developed a high degree of respect for each other. When K. S. came to the United States in 1947, the Rev. Hoeksema was recuperating from a stroke at his home and much of his physical strength (he had been a blacksmith in his younger days) was broken. Schilder again traveled from coast to coast, as he had done in 1939. This time, however, he spoke mostly in the Protestant Reformed churches. The crowds were smaller than eight years before because most of the Protestant Reformed churches had few members. Many CRC ministers and church members also went to hear him when he was in their neighborhood. It was a treat for many to hear the brilliant Dutch theologian once more.

Again he published a journal of his travels in *De Reformatie*. From his experiences on his visit, he began to suspect that the synodical leaders of the GKN exercised a degree of influence on the CRC. This saddened him, because he felt that it could only lead to greater difficulties in the CRC in the future. His lectures on the church were not only well received, but those who could understand him realized that he was addressing a vital subject, because there were leaders in the churches who no longer seemed to know what the concept "church" meant. K. S. maintained that if the biblical and confessional (e.g., Articles 27–32 of the Belgic Confession) teachings about the church were not understood, then it would also be difficult to have a proper appreciation for office, worship, and ecumenicity. His insights alerted his audiences to the dangers confronting the churches.

Chapter 5
The Final Years

While Schilder was in the United States, Prof. Greijdanus and Prof. Veenhof tended to the work connected with *De Reformatie*. When he returned to the Netherlands, he took on the full load himself. He began a rather lengthy discussion in print with Rev. Hoeksema concerning the doctrine of common grace. Hoeksema had been deposed as a minister of the CRC because hè denied this doctrine. Schilder did not agree with Hoeksema, but neither did he agree with the three points drawn up by the CRC synod of 1924—points that opposed the position of Hoeksema and articulated the CRC's own stand. Schilder thought it was a mistake to begin with the ideas of election and reprobation in the discussion of common grace. He preferred to go back to the idea of the common mandate given to Adam and Eve in paradise. Worthwhile material may be found in the issues of *De Reformatie* in which Hoeksema and Schilder debated the topic.

Later, however, when they began to speak of the presence or absence of conditions in the covenant—a debate that led to a split among the Protestant Reformed churches, Schilder wrote that he was finished with this matter. Until this time he had urged Dutch church members who emigrated to either Canada or the United States to affiliate with the Protestant Reformed churches rather than with the CRC. The Protestant Reformed churches received many sincere and capable members from the "liberated" churches. Now, however, when he bade Rev. Hoeksema farewell, he urged the emigrating members to establish their own churches. From these circumstances, the Canadian Reformed churches took their origin.

Often the Canadian Reformed churches are viewed as an extension of the "liberated" churches in Holland. This is not correct, even though there is a very close association between the two. The "liberated" churches in Holland are really the mother churches of the Canadian Reformed and American Reformed churches. The Canadian Reformed churches form a federation of their own. They have an excellent theological school for the training of their ministers at Hamilton, Ontario. Besides, they have their own teachers' college and elementary and high schools in various parts of Canada. Most of their churches are located in Canada, but there are a few in the United States. They publish their own magazine, the *Clarion*. It is a small denomination but one which has remained true to the Scriptures and the confessions and has exerted influence far greater than its number of members might lead one to expect.

The first breach in the ranks of the "liberated" in the Netherlands came in 1948 when Prof. S. Greijdanus passed away. He had taught New Testament theology since 1922. He was a man of uncommon ability, and his writings have retained their value through the years. He had retired in 1939, and the synod meeting that year had appointed Dr. H. Ridderbos as his successor. The writings of both Schilder and Greijdanus made it quite evident that they were not pleased with the appointment of Ridderbos nor with the way in which it was made. Greijdanus had come out of retirement in 1945 to join Schilder at the new Kampen theological school. Schilder lost a close friend and a "father" when this scholar passed away. Greijdanus's huge library and his whole estate were willed to the school. The library at the liberated theological school in Kampen was greatly enriched by all the books—many of them priceless—that Greijdanus had accumulated during his long lifetime. Greijdanus was childless but made his students his "sons."

As the "liberated" churches saw it, the situation in the GKN did not improve. The wrong move had been made in the dogmatic constructions the synod had adopted in 1944, and the effects of its action were soon evident not only in the numbers lost to the denomination, but also in the character of the church that survived. Leaders began to "play around" with the doctrines adopted in 1944. At the time every officer had to sign his agreement with the denominational doctrines or stand in danger of losing his office. After just two years, the synod itself overturned the decisions of 1944. A "pastoral letter" had been sent to all the churches in 1944, urging them to pray for a blessing on the decision of synod to depose Dr. Schilder.

A short time later, professors, ministers, and candidates for the ministry were given far greater leeway for the doctrinal formulations that had been in dispute and still remained in good official standing. The effect on the churches was catastrophic. Respect for denominational leaders and decisions of major assemblies fell precipitously. Through the exodus of the "liberated," many local churches had lost their leaders and/or their best members. During the war the GKN churches were filled with worshipers twice every Sunday. Soon afterwards many were almost empty. The GKN had defended the authority of the Scriptures from its earliest days. Now fundamental questions about traditional stands were asked. The confessions were no longer honored as they had been before; rather, greater latitude was permitted.

Was this all due to the rupture that took place in the denomination in 1944? No doubt other factors also entered the equation, but the split in the churches, precipitated by the synod in 1944, played an important role in the rapid decline of the GKN. Dr. Schilder was denied a place in the GKN because, it was charged, he was not Reformed. Yet others were allowed in the denomination's pulpits even though they denied almost every Reformed tenet. Few men had done as much as K. S. had for the welfare of the churches and the development of true Reformed doctrine and polity, but the GKN turned its back to him and placed him outside its walls.

It was not long after the ecclesiastical "liberation" that a movement began to reunite the broken pieces of the GKN. The first attempts were made by that part of the church that had now often been termed the "synodical" element. This was the part that considered itself the continuation of the Reformed churches. Church leaders realized that they had suffered a terrible blow in 1944. None of them had dreamt that the exodus from the denomination would attain such proportions. Many of the leading ministers and most astute theologians had left at the time when Schilder and Greijdanus were deposed. Overtures were made to several ministers of the "liberated" churches that talks should be begun between them and the synodicals. A request even came to the synod of the "liberated" churches asking for discussions aimed at unification.

Naturally there could be no objection to conversations meant to bring like-minded Christians together institutionally. Schilder had always taught that ecumenicity should be practiced among believers who accepted the same confessions. The "liberated" synod agreed to talks *if* they were accompanied by written statements from both sides outlining clearly and precisely any differences of opinion. Schilder was afraid of talks without written guidance. He had seen too much of this in the past. He felt that soon after such talks would come to an end, no one would know the exact meaning of the statements they had discussed. Only if the points at issue were available in written form would there be the proper safeguards. The synod of the GKN understood the desire for written documents to be a restriction and received the impression that the "liberated" churches really did not wish to talk. They held that there should be a cordial atmosphere at a round table where all differences could be discussed.

Since the "liberated" synod would not initiate talks without written documents, the GKN decided to proceed in a different

97

manner. Contact was made with several ministers of the "liberated" churches, and they were invited to conferences at which the differences between the two sides were to be aired. It was also made clear that the doctrinal formulations of 1944 did not have to be a stumbling block. Those formulations had accomplished their purpose, and it was felt that further progress might now be possible if each side would confess some wrongdoing in 1944 and then unite as though nothing had happened.

A few ministers accepted the invitation. One of them was Rev. B. A. Bos, an officer at the first synod of the "liberated" churches. There was some correspondence between Schilder and Rev. Bos in the pages of *De Reformatie*. Schilder warned him what was at stake. But Rev. Bos returned to the GKN, and a considerable number of people went with him. Rev. Bos did not find a home in the GKN as he had hoped but later left the denomination and became a minister in the *Christelijke Gereformeerde Kerk*. There were a few more defections from the "liberated" churches in the late 1940s. But the number of new members who joined them was far greater than the total of those who left. The "liberated" churches continued to grow.

The year 1949 was the thirty-fifth anniversary of K. S.'s ordination as a minister of the gospel. He did not celebrate the day because he never celebrated any day or event that concerned himself. However, the other editors of his paper schemed with the publisher to put out an edition of the paper that took due note of this important day in his life and in the life of the churches. Whenever something like this happened, K. S. was embarrassed that so much was made of an event in his life, but he was also as pleased as a little child. That was typically Klaas Schilder! His way of thinking was: Let us not make too much of what an individual has accomplished; rather, let us continue the huge volume of work that remains to be done in the church of our Lord and Savior. He was a true son of the church and a beloved friend of all those who knew him well.

98

Schilder worked without respite as long as he had the strength to do it. He realized that much was at stake. He was the acknowledged leader of the "liberated" churches, and people looked to him for guidance. He was also fully aware of the dangers surrounding the "liberated" churches. He knew there would be more defections because the enticements from the GKN were considerable. The "liberation" in 1944 had emphasized the autonomy of the local churches—the visible church. He had a clear view of what was meant by this autonomy of the local churches because he had a clear conception of the meaning of *church* in the Scriptures and in the confessions.

However, not everyone had as clear a grasp of the concept as he did. Some leaders of the "liberation" became extremists in their view of the church. They agreed with K. S. in his interpretation of the last part of Article 31 of the church order—that one was not required to obey the decisions of a synod if they contradict either the Bible or the church order. But some felt that the autonomy of the local church would also release them from the first part of Article 31—a clause dealing with the power of broader church assemblies to make decisions for all the churches. Then a synod has no place because nothing is "settled and binding." Their emphases led to an independentism, which plagued the "liberated" churches a few years later when a sizable element left. Although not intended, the seeds for the *Buiten Verband* (= Union of those outside) group could be found soon after the "liberation." The "liberated" churches suffered a major loss when two of their Kampen professors—Veenhof and Jager—joined the seceders.

Around 1950, K. S. saw difficulties surfacing. The church had done well since 1944 and had achieved a size that no one had expected at the beginning. Yet storm clouds were beginning to appear. The cohesiveness of the early days was slowly disappearing. Was the work of so many years to be in vain? K. S. did not believe so because he was convinced that he had taken the right step in 1944. He worked doubly hard to minimize the effect that GKN publications from around 1950 might have on the members of the church. He taught. He pleaded. He warned. His work had its desired effect because he still had the confidence of the churches. The people loved him, and they had the highest respect for his great ability. They read his paper every week, and many tried to understand the books he had written—not an easy task. He had also resumed his writing on the Heidelberg Catechism soon after the liberation.

On March 23, 1952, Dr. Prof. Klaas Schilder died after suffering a massive heart attack. The day of his death fell exactly eight years after the GKN synod had suspended him from office. In the last copy of *De Reformatie* that he edited, he notified his readers that his medical doctor had ordered him to rest for a while. Nothing serious, he assured them; he just needed some rest and everything would be all right. The next issue of the paper was bordered in black because the editor had already passed away. He was only sixty-one years of age.

Even in death the lines were drawn sharply around Schilder. The GKN writers took note of his death and stated that he had gone home. A harmless expression? Hardly. His own family as well as Prof. Holwerda reacted strongly. They wondered how editorialists of the GKN publications could speak of his "going home" when they had expelled him as being unworthy of membership in the church here on earth. Somewhat the same sentiments had been voiced in 1948 when Prof. Greijdanus died. Then one of the "old" Kampen professors wrote that Greijdanus had always remained "one of them." Then, too, the family had reacted very negatively. The former colleagues of Greijdanus at the Kampen theological school were not welcome at the family home nor at the funeral. Church splits had left deep wounds.

What more can be said about Schilder? He was perhaps the greatest Reformed theologian of the twentieth century. He was a scholar who left a rich legacy for all those who are able and desire to read his works. He was a man who loved his Lord and His church. He loved the Reformed faith and did much to defend and develop it. He loved his family and his friends. He did not sail under a false flag. The GKN Synod of 1988 finally acknowledged that the church had made a mistake in 1944 when it suspended and later deposed Schilder.

Epilogue

Was the situation of 1944 worth a split in the church? Many would say no. If we look at the sorrow it caused in so many families and the disruption of the fine work done unitedly for many years in so many areas of endeavor, we would be inclined to agree. But the blame must be placed where it belongs—at the door of the GKN. Unity is a precious commodity in the church. Our Lord has instructed His people to pray and work for it. However, the truth may not be sacrificed or compromised. Truth and unity may not be played off against each other.

If we consider that the church of Abraham Kuyper and Herman Bavinck deposed a thoroughly Reformed leader like Klaas Schilder but allows the deviations from the Reformed faith as they are practiced today, we begin to see the purpose of the liberation. Its existence guarantees that there is at least one group of churches that still upholds the historic Reformed beliefs. The GKN has allowed leaders to deny the historicity of the first eleven chapters of Genesis and to question the resurrection and even atonement through the blood of Christ without disciplining them. As a result, in many places the members of the churches are fed stones instead of bread. Morality and lifestyle are no longer judged by the law of God but by the modern standards of society.

In contrast, the liberated churches have continued to uphold a view of Scripture that agrees with the confessions of the church. As a result, these churches are filled with worshipers on Sunday, and they still enjoy a vital religious life. From this point of view, yes, despite all the pain that resulted from the breach made in the churches, it was worth it. The historic Reformed faith is preached and believed. A heritage has been preserved to transmit to the coming generations. The liberated churches have erected a system of schools that honors the teachings of the word of God. This denomination is indeed the continuation of the historic Reformed churches.

The history of the Reformed churches in the Netherlands is of more than passing interest for those who embrace the same faith in America. History must teach us. Developments in the GKN from 1936 to 1944 led to a revision of the way in which the denomination exercised its disciplinary supervision of its officers. Authority was removed from the local to the regional and national levels. The new disciplinary system was applied at least in part to handle Schilder and the difficulties he posed. Discipline, however unpopular it has become, is, according to the Heidelberg Catechism, one of the keys of the kingdom. If the faithful exercise of ecclesiastical supervision is lost or distorted, the churches have lost a basic feature of their systems. That is what happened in the GKN during the war years, and the results are evident for all to see. If we listen, we will be the wiser.

References

Literature to Consult

Works of K. Schilder

Christ in His Suffering. Grand Rapids: Wm. B. Eerdmans, 1938. *Christ on Trial*. Grand Rapids: Wm. B. Eerdmans, 1939. *Christ Crucified*. Grand Rapids: Wm. B. Eerdmans, 1940. (All three volumes of the trilogy were translated from the Dutch by Dr. H. Zylstra.)

Christus en Cultuur. Franeker: T. Wever, 1953.

Gereformeerd Farizeisme? Delft: W. D. Meinema, 1925.

Heidelbergsche Catechismus. Goes: Oosterbaan & Le Cointre, 1939.

Licht in den Rook. Delft: W. D. Meinema, 1923.

Openbaring van Johannes en het Sociale Level, De. Delft: W. D. Meinema, 1924.

Reformatie, De. vols. 1–28 (1920–1951). Goes: Oosterbaan & Le Cointre.

Tusschen "Ja en Neen." Kampen: J. H. Kok, 1929.

Wat is de Hel? Kampen: J. H. Kok, 1920.

Wat is de Hemel? Kampen: J. H. Kok, 1935.

Other Works

Berkouwer, G. C. *Zoeken en Vinden*. Kampen: J. H. Kok.

Bos, C. G. *Nederlandse Kergeschiedenis na 1945* . Groningen: De Vuurbaak, 1980.

Jongeling, P., J. P. De Vrres, and J. Douma. *Het vuur blijft branden.* Kampen: J. H. Kok, 1979.

Lindeboom, A.M. *De Theologen Gingen Voorop.* Kampen: J. H. Kok, 1987.

Praamsma, L. *Het Dwaze Gods.* Wageningen: Zomer en Keuning, Uitgeversmaatschappij, 1950.

Van Reest, R. *Opdat Zij; Allen Een Zijn,* 2 vols. Goes: Oosterbaan & Le Cointre, 1962.

——. *Schilder's Struggle for the Unity of the Church.* Translated by T. Plantinga. Neerlandia: Inheritance Publications, 1962.

Van Reest, R. *Terugzien na Vijfentwintig Jaren.* Goes: Oosterbaan & Le Cointre, 1972.

The few books mentioned above will aid the reader in further study of K. Schilder and in the study of the history of the Reformed churches in the Netherlands during this important period of time.